THE
Vegetarian
COOKBOOK

THE
Vegetarian
COOKBOOK

FROM EARTH TO TABLE

CONSULTANT EDITORS
NICOLA GRAIMES AND FIONA BIGGS

This edition published in 2011
LOVE FOOD is an imprint of Parragon Books Ltd

Parragon
Queen Street House
4 Queen Street
Bath BA1 1HE, UK

ISBN: 978-1-4454-3813-9

Printed in China

Internal Design by Talking Design
Consultant editors Nicola Graimes and Fiona Biggs
Photography by Mike Cooper
Illustrations by Coral Mula
Home Economy by Lincoln Jefferson

NOTES FOR THE READER
This book uses both metric and imperial measurements. Follow the same units of measurement throughout; do not mix
metric and imperial. All spoon measurements are level: teaspoons are assumed to be 5 ml, and tablespoons are assumed
to be 15 ml. Unless otherwise stated, milk is assumed to be full fat, eggs and individual vegetables are medium, and pepper
is freshly ground black pepper.

The times given are an approximate guide only. Preparation times differ according to the techniques used by different people
and the cooking times may also vary from those given. Optional ingredients, variations or serving suggestions have not been
included in the calculations.

Recipes using raw or very lightly cooked eggs should be avoided by infants, the elderly, pregnant women, convalescents and
anyone suffering from an illness. Pregnant and breastfeeding women are advised to avoid eating peanuts and peanut products.
Sufferers from nut allergies should be aware that some of the ready-made ingredients used in the recipes in this book may
contain nuts. Always check the packaging before use.

Vegetarians should be aware that some of the ready-prepared ingredients used in the recipes in this book may contain animal
products. Always check the packaging before use.

Picture Acknowledgements
The publisher would like to thank the following for permission to reproduce copyright material on the following pages:
front cover image. Assortment of vegetables in bowl © Rita Maas/Getty Images

CONTENTS

INTRODUCTION

The Vegetarian Cookbook is a comprehensive guide to preparing, cooking and serving a vast range of vegetables, pulses, nuts and seeds. The directories at the front of each chapter introduce the fabulous variety of vegetarian food – a far cry from the days when there was very little choice of vegetables on offer and when vegetarianism was regarded as something of a fad. The recipes in this book, inspired by cuisines of places as diverse as North Africa and China, cater for every meal type and occasion, from quick snacks and dips to hearty main courses, and from delicious salads to hearty meal-in-a-bowl soups.

WHAT IS A VEGETARIAN?

The plant-based vegetarian diet is enjoyed by millions of people around the world, people as diverse as the variety of fruit and vegetables on offer at your local greengrocer's or supermarket.

The most basic definition of a vegetarian is someone who doesn't eat meat, poultry, game, fish, shellfish or other seafood, or the by-products of slaughter, such as gelatine or animal fats. Most vegetarians choose to get their nutrients from a diet of fruit and vegetables, grains, nuts, pulses and seeds. Some vegetarians also include dairy products and eggs.

While some vegetarians make this choice for ethical and moral reasons and others for religious reasons, many vegetarians simply enjoy the culinary pleasure of eating lots of flavoursome, fresh vegetables and fruit. Whatever the reasons, however, the popularity of vegetarianism is increasing and no longer carries the stigma of being a weird, alternative lifestyle that it once had in Western countries. And whatever reason you have for wanting vegetarian recipes, you'll find a mouthwatering selection in this collection.

Types of vegetarian

Just as the plant world offers much variety, the vegetarian diet comes in many guises. These are some of the most common vegetarian choices:

Fruitarian These vegetarians eat mostly raw fruit, grains and nuts, in the belief that only plant foods that can be harvested without killing a plant should be eaten.

Lacto-vegetarian Dairy products, but no eggs, are included in this diet. This style of vegetarianism provides a lot of culinary scope in the kitchen because it includes cheese, cream, milk and yogurt.

Lacto-ovo-vegetarian Dairy products and eggs are included in this diet, providing great variety at mealtimes. This is the most common form of vegetarianism and all the recipes in this book are suitable for this lifestyle.

Macrobiotic vegetarian This is a diet usually followed for spiritual and philosophical reasons, which aims to maintain a balance between foods seen as yin (positive) and yang (negative).

Vegan This is a vegetarian whose daily diet doesn't include any dairy products or eggs. Although many millions of people around the world are vegan, this isn't always the straightforward choice it appears to be. Vegans must become diligent label readers to avoid the less-than-obvious butter and eggs in many prepared foods. One reason oriental stir-fries and stews are so popular with vegans is because the staple rice and mung-bean noodles are not made with eggs, as Italian pasta is.

Becoming a vegetarian

If you are new to eating a meatless diet, it can be comforting to know that many familiar, everyday dishes are, in fact, vegetarian, especially if you decide to adopt a lacto-ovo diet. Jot down a list of all your favourite meals and chances are you'll find some that easily fit your new diet, for example beans on toast, scrambled eggs and toasted cheese sandwiches. You'll find everyday favourites in this global collection of recipes that you might already enjoy eating as an omnivore, such as Pasta Salad with Chargrilled Peppers, Creamy Mushroom & Tarragon Soup, Pasta with Pesto, Roasted Root Vegetables. Take-away favourites, such as Aubergine Curry and Sesame Hot Noodles, for example, can also feature in vegetarian meals. You will quickly appreciate how old-fashioned the idea is that vegetarians eat only brown rice and salad leaves!

If becoming a vegetarian means a radical overhaul of all your cooking and eating habits, make the change gradually. Rather than trying to change a lifetime of eating habits overnight, start by simply cutting out red meat for a couple of weeks, then go on to eliminating fish and shellfish and, finally, poultry. Then you can carry on slowly eliminating dairy products or other foods as you wish. This approach will also help you to avoid cravings.

Try to cook something new two or three times a week. Highlight recipes in this collection that you've never tried before and you will soon discover how varied and delicious a vegetarian diet can be.

HEALTH BENEFITS

Humans have always eaten plant-based diets and today most of the world's population eats a vegetarian or near-vegetarian diet. More people are adopting a meat-free lifestyle every day. Many and varied reasons fuel this expansion of vegetarianism around the globe. Religious conviction and the belief that a vegetarian diet is a healthy choice are the deciding factors for many, but for others the conversion to vegetarianism come from the desire to eat well for less money, concern about the environment and worries over the more-numerous-than-ever food scares. For many vegetarians, it is, quite simply, an ethical decision not to kill animals.

Whatever your reasons for becoming a vegetarian, you will undoubtedly find that vegetarianism offers great scope and choice at mealtimes. Along with many favourite Western dishes you'll find inspiration for meals from cultures around the world in the delicious collection of recipes in this book. India and China have large vegetarian populations, but flavoursome recipe ideas from Africa, the rest of South-East Asia, the Middle East and the countries bordering the Mediterranean are also included.

Health benefits of going green

One of the great appeals of a vegetarian diet, especially in the West, is that you don't eat any of the saturated fats found in animal products that have been linked with some of the most deadly diseases of the twenty-first century, such as heart disease and various forms of cancer.

Unfortunately, a vegetarian diet in itself won't guarantee optimum health. If you simply replace the meat in your old diet with cheese and full-fat milk, for example, which are both high in saturated fat, you might not see much improvement. And, likewise, if you try to live on a diet of just brown rice, tofu and beansprouts you won't be getting the nutrients you need for a healthy body – these are discussed in the following pages.

There is no doubt, however, that a vegetarian diet will go a long way towards meeting today's many nutritional guidelines. As a vegetarian you will almost certainly eat more than the recommended five portions of fruit and vegetables a day, so, if you make smart changes, you should eliminate many of the potential health problems associated with a meat-based diet. A varied vegetarian diet will also be higher in fibre, which is believed to help prevent constipation, bowel disorders and other serious health problems. Some studies have also determined that obesity, with its numerous health complications, is less of a problem for vegetarians than it is for meat-eaters.

Despite all the confusing – and often conflicting – advice about healthy eating, the one thing nutritionists agree on is that eating at least five portions, or 400 g/ 14 oz, of fruit and vegetables every day forms the backbone of a healthy diet. Plant foods are a powerhouse of essential nutrients – these include B vitamins, especially important for women planning a family; vitamin C for general immunity and healing; powerful antioxidants that reduce the risk of heart diseases, cancer, cataracts, arthritis and sperm damage. Antioxidants also reduce some of the problems associated with ageing by fighting free radicals that are caused by pollutants in the environment and as a by-product of natural cell functions. This is why a vegetarian diet can be instrumental in your overall well-being.

A religious choice

Some religions, who believe in reincarnation, are prohibited by their religious beliefs from eating meat. For many vegetarians, avoiding heavy food, such as red meat, is regarded as a step towards spiritual enlightenment. They believe that consuming lighter, less dense food allows an individual to reach a higher state of consciousness.

A lifestyle choice

In light of the all-too-frequent health scares, such as those over CJD (Creutzfeldt-Jacob disease), caused by eating meat from cows with BSE (bovine spongiform encephalopathy), and avian flu in poultry, the changeover to a meat-free diet provides peace of mind for many converts to vegetarianism. Vegetarianism is also believed to reduce the likelihood of potentially fatal illness from bacterial infections, such as *E. coli* in meat or salmonella in eggs.

Food hygiene

Eating and cooking with only plant-based ingredients, however, doesn't automatically give you a clean bill of health. Food hygiene is just as important as it is when cooking with animal products. Unless your ingredients are organic, it is advisable to wash them thoroughly before cooking to remove any pesticide residue. You can buy a special solution for washing fruit and vegetables from health food stores and some supermarkets.

THE IMPORTANCE OF A BALANCED DIET

Vegetarians, just like meat-eaters, need a variety of nutrients on a daily basis in order to function in tip-top form and remain healthy. And it is only by eating a wide variety of foods every day that you get all the nutrients you need naturally. If, for example, you eat a selection of green, red, yellow and orange fruit and vegetables at each meal you will probably be getting all the essential nutrients. If, however, you look at your plate and see only brown and beige, it is time to rethink your menu planning. Beetroot Salad, Radiatori with Pumpkin Sauce, Carrot & Orange Stir-Fry and Sweet Potato & Apple Soup are just a few of the colourful recipes that will help you along the road to healthy eating.

Variety for health

The Vegetarian Society of Great Britain recommends the following food choices for your daily diet:

- 4–5 servings of fruit and vegetables
- 3–4 servings of cereals and/or grains or potatoes
- 2–3 servings of nuts, seeds and pulses
- 2 servings of milk, cheese, eggs or soya products
- small amount of vegetable oil, margarine or butter
- yeast extract, such as Marmite, fortified with vitamin B12

If that looks like a huge amount of food, it isn't. Something as simple and as satisfying as Leek & Goat's Cheese Crêpes, for example, provides at least one serving from four of the categories. When you want a snack, try a jacket potato topped with grated cheese or a handful of toasted nuts and you'll be well on your way to reaching the daily target.

The goodness in food

All the food you eat contains a combination of proteins, carbohydrates and fats – you need a balanced mixture of each every day to stay healthy.

Protein, made up of amino acids, is essential for the growth, development and maintenance and repair of cells.

Unfortunately, soya products are the only non-animal foods that contain all the essential amino acids. That is why it is so important to eat a variety of food every day, although if you include cheese, eggs, cow's milk and yogurt in your diet you are less at risk of being protein-deficient. Good sources of protein include all soya products, such as tofu, soya milk and commercial textured vegetable protein, pulses, whole grains and cereals, nuts and seeds, and butter, cheese, cow's milk and eggs.

Carbohydrates give you energy. They can be either simple or complex, and it is the complex carbohydrates that are most nutritionally beneficial, containing a mix of vitamins and minerals and releasing the energy you need slowly, so that you will feel the benefits for longer. Sweet Potato & Apple Soup and Chickpea Hotpot are examples of delicious dishes that supply generous amounts of complex carbohydrates. Good sources are almost all fruit and vegetables, especially root vegetables, potatoes and bananas; pulses; and whole grains, cereals, rice and pasta.

What Is a Serving?

- 100 ml/3½ fl oz fruit juice (only one glass a day counts)
- 1 medium fruit or vegetable, such as an apple, orange or onion
- 3 heaped tablespoons of fresh or canned fruit salad, sliced carrots or mushrooms or cooked lentils
- 1 tablespoon of raisins or sultanas, or 4 dried apricots, or a handful of banana chips

Despite the modern tendency to look at anything labelled 'low-fat' as beneficial, a small amount of fat in your diet is needed to feel well and look good. Most of the fat that comes from animal products, however, is saturated and commonly known as the 'bad' fat because of the links with serious diseases. 'Good' fats, which are called polyunsaturated or monosaturated, come from vegetable plants, for example olive and sunflower oils, and these are the ones you should use in cooking and salad dressings.

One of the bonuses of eating a vegetarian diet is that most fruits and vegetables are very low in saturated fat, and the high-fat plant foods, such as avocados, olives, nuts and seeds, contain the 'good' fats. Polyunsaturated or monounsaturated fats are those that come from vegetable sources, for example olive and sunflower oils. Avoid anything with palm oil on the label.

Vitamins for vegans

Anyone adopting a vegan diet should consult a qualified nutritionist or GP. Vitamin B12, essential for healthy red blood cells, is lacking in a vegan diet. Vegans should consider taking a B12 supplement or eat soya products supplemented with B12.

ESSENTIAL VITAMINS AND MINERALS

VITAMIN/MINERAL	FUNCTION	GOOD VEGETARIAN SOURCES	PROBLEMS CAUSED BY DEFICIENCY
VITAMIN A (retinol in animal foods, beta carotene in plant foods)	For healthy vision, bone growth, skin and tissue repair. Beta carotene acts as an antioxidant and supports the immune system	Dairy products, egg yolk, margarine, carrots, apricots, squash, red peppers, broccoli, green leafy vegetables, mangoes, dried apricots and sweet potatoes	Poor night vision, dry skin and impaired immune system, especially respiratory disorders
VITAMIN B$_1$ (thiamine)	Essential for breaking down carbohydrates, protecting the nervous system, muscles and heart, promoting growth and boosting mental well-being	Wholegrain cereals, brewer's yeast, yeast extract, Brazil nuts, sunflower seeds, peanuts, rice, bran and mycoprotein (Quorn®)	Depression, irritability, nervous disorders, memory loss. Common among alcoholics
VITAMIN B$_2$ (riboflavin)	Essential for energy production, healthy skin, tissue repair and maintenance	Cheese, eggs, milk, yogurt, fortified breakfast cereals, yeast extract, almonds, wholemeal bread, mushrooms, prunes, cashew nuts and pumpkin seeds	Lack of energy, skin problems, dry cracked lips, numbness and itchy eyes
VITAMIN B$_3$ (niacin)	Essential for energy production, healthy digestive system, skin and nervous system	Pulses, yeast extract, potatoes, fortified breakfast cereals, wheatgerm, peanuts, cheese, eggs, mushrooms, green leafy vegetables, figs, prunes and sesame seeds	Deficiency is unusual, but is characterized by lack of energy, depression and scaly skin
VITAMIN B$_6$ (pyridoxine)	Essential for assimilating protein and fat, red blood cell formation and a healthy immune system	Eggs, wheatgerm, wholemeal flour, yeast extract, breakfast cereals, peanuts, bananas, currants and lentils	Anaemia, dermatitis and depression
VITAMIN B$_{12}$ (cyanocobalamin)	Essential for red blood cell formation, growth, healthy nervous system and energy production	Dairy products, eggs, fortified breakfast cereals, cheese, yeast extract, fortified soya milk	Fatigue, poor resistance to infection, breathlessness and anaemia
Folate (folic acid)	Essential for red blood cell formation, making genetic material (DNA) and protein synthesis. Extra is needed pre-conception and during pregnancy to protect the foetus against neural tube defects	Green leafy vegetables, broccoli, fortified breakfast cereals, bread, nuts, pulses, bananas, yeast extract and asparagus	Anaemia and appetite loss; also linked to neural defects in babies
VITAMIN C (ascorbic acid)	Essential for healthy skin, teeth, bones, gums, immune system, resistance to infection, energy production and growth	Citrus fruit, melons, strawberries, tomatoes, broccoli, potatoes, peppers and green leafy vegetables	Impaired immune system, fatigue, insomnia and depression
VITAMIN D	Essential for healthy teeth and bones; aids absorption of calcium and phosphate	Sunlight, non-hydrogenated vegetable margarine, vegetable oils, eggs and dairy products	Bone and muscle weakness. Long-term shortage results in rickets

VITAMIN/MINERAL	FUNCTION	GOOD VEGETARIAN SOURCES	PROBLEMS CAUSED BY DEFICIENCY
VITAMIN E (tocopherol)	Essential for healthy skin, circulation and cell maintenance. As an antioxidant, it protects vitamins A and C in the body	Seeds, wheatgerm, nuts, vegetable oils, eggs, wholemeal bread, green leafy vegetables, oats, sunflower oil, avocado and fortified breakfast cereals	Increased risk of heart disease, strokes and certain cancers
VITAMIN K	Essential for effective blood clotting	Spinach, cabbage and cauliflower	Deficiency is rare
Calcium	Essential for building and maintaining bones and teeth, muscle function and the nervous system	Dairy products, green leafy vegetables, sesame seeds, broccoli, dried fruit, pulses, almonds, spinach, watercress and tofu	Soft and brittle bones, osteoporosis, fractures and muscle weakness
Iron	Essential component of haemoglobin, which transports oxygen in the blood	Egg yolk, fortified breakfast cereals, green leafy vegetables, dried fruit, cashew nuts, pulses, wholegrains, tofu, pumpkin seeds, black treacle and brown rice	Anaemia, fatigue and low resistance to infection
Magnesium	Essential for healthy muscles, bones and teeth, normal growth and energy production	Nuts, seeds, wholegrains, pulses, tofu, dried figs, dried apricots and green vegetables	Deficiency rare, but characterized by lethargy, weak bones and muscles, depression and irritability
Phosphorus	Essential for healthy bones and teeth, muscle function, energy production and the assimilation of nutrients, particularly calcium	Found in most foods: milk, cheese, yogurt, eggs, nuts, seeds, pulses and wholegrains	Deficiency is rare
Potassium	Important in maintaining the body's water balance, normal blood pressure and nerve transmission	Bananas, milk, pulses, nuts, seeds, wholegrains, potatoes, fruit and root vegetables	Weakness, thirst, fatigue, mental confusion and raised blood pressure
Selenium	Essential for protecting against free radical damage and for red blood cell function as well as healthy hair and skin	Avocados, lentils, milk, cheese, wholemeal bread, cashew nuts, walnuts, seaweed and sunflower seeds	Reduced immunity
Zinc	Essential for a healthy immune system, tissue formation, normal growth, wound healing and reproduction	Peanuts, cheese, wholegrains, sunflower and pumpkin seeds, pulses, milk, hard cheese, yogurt, wheatgerm and mycoprotein (Quorn®)	Impaired growth and development, slow wound healing and loss of sense of taste and smell

PLANNING MEALS

The key to a good diet is variety – serving the same meals every week will soon dull even the most enthusiastic palate. A balanced meal is one that combines sufficient amounts of protein, carbohydrate, fibre, the right types of fat, vitamins and minerals. The ideal diet includes enough calories to provide the body with the vital energy it needs, but not an excess, which leads to weight gain.

Keeping a meal balanced

Make sure each meal contains a protein (eggs, pulses, tofu, dairy products, nuts and seeds) and a carbohydrate (pasta, rice, wholegrains, bread) element. Despite the current popularity of low-carb diets, it is recommended that at least 50 per cent of a meal is carbohydrate based. Remember that many foods, such as pulses and wholegrains, are a combination of protein and carbohydrate. A moderate amount of fat in the diet is essential, not only for health, but also as it contributes to the taste, texture and palatability of food. Restrict fat levels to no more than 30 per cent of your daily diet and stick to polyunsaturated fats.

Try to include at least two different types of cooked vegetable (steamed, stir-fried, microwaved or roasted, rather than boiled) in the main meal, or prepare a large salad that combines a range of different types of different-coloured vegetables such as rocket, watercress, spinach, beetroot, avocado, tomatoes and carrot. Fruit or fruit-based desserts make a perfect and convenient end to a meal or low-fat snack.

Try not to stick to the same meals every week. Experiment with different foods and try out new recipes. Before you do your weekly shop, either write down or mentally prepare a week's repertoire of meals. In this way, you can ensure that you eat a range of different foods and that you will have the correct ingredients to hand rather than a collection of foods that do not work together.

It is a common misconception that vegetarians have to meticulously combine protein foods in every meal to achieve the correct balance of amino acids. The latest expert advice states that, provided you eat a varied range of vegetarian protein foods on a daily basis, this is sufficient; intentionally combining proteins is unnecessary.

Vegetarian Children

There is no reason why children should not thrive on a vegetarian diet – as long as it is not based on cheese sandwiches, beans and chips. However, they do have slightly different dietary requirements from adults. Young children can find fibre difficult to digest in large amounts; too much can make them feel full before they have been able to ingest enough nutrients and can lead to stomach upsets. Fibre can also interfere with the absorption of iron, zinc and calcium. Refined bran should not be added to a young child's diet. Reduced-fat foods, such as skimmed milk and low-fat cheese, lack the much-needed calories and therefore energy required by young growing children: reduced-fat dairy products are suitable for children over two years, but younger children require the full-fat equivalent. Parents are also advised to give their children at least five portions of fruit and vegetables a day, but this should be divided as three portions of fruit and two of vegetables – fruit provides plenty of energy. Babies and young children do not have the capacity to eat large amounts of food and so need to eat three small nutritious meals a day, plus two healthy snacks.

Watch Out For...

It is always wise to check food and drink labels when shopping. The following checklist makes a useful reference guide.

ADDITIVES
These include emulsifiers, colourings and flavourings, and may or may not be vegetarian. Two of the most common are E441 (gelatine), a gelling agent derived from animal parts and bones, and E120 (cochineal), made from crushed insects.

ALBUMEN
Albumen may be derived from battery-farmed eggs.

ALCOHOL
Alcohol is clarified using animal ingredients. All cask-conditioned 'real' ales, and some bottled, canned and keg bitters, milds and stouts are fined (clarified) with isinglass derived from the swim bladders of certain tropical fish. Wine may also be fined with isinglass, dried blood, egg albumen derived from battery hens, gelatine and chitin from crab and shrimp shells. Vegetarian alternatives include bentonite, kieselguhr, kaolin and silica gel. Non-vintage port is fined with gelatine.

ANIMAL FATS
Animal fats are sometimes found in biscuits, cakes, pastry, stock, chips, margarine, ready meals, margarine and ice cream. Edible fats can mean animal fats.

ASPIC
Aspic is a savoury jelly derived from meat or fish.

CHEESE
Many cheeses are produced using animal rennet, an enzyme taken from the stomach of a calf. Vegetarian cheese is made using microbial or fungal enzymes. Non-vegetarian cheese is often used in pesto, sauces and ready meals.

EGGS
Eggs are animal products. Some foods, such as mayonnaise or pasta, may contain battery-farmed eggs. If possible, try to buy organic free-range eggs.

GRAVY
Gravy is made from meat juices, although vegetarian gravy mixes do exist.

JELLY
Jelly usually contains animal-derived gelatine, but it is possible to buy vegetarian alternatives set with agar-agar or guar gum.

MARGARINE
Margarine may contain animal-derived vitamin D3, fats, gelatine and E numbers as well as whey.

SOFT DRINKS
Soft drinks, particularly canned orange drinks, may contain gelatine, which is used as a carrier for added beta carotene.

SOUP
Soup may contain animal stock or fat.

SUET
Suet is animal fat, but vegetarian versions do exist.

SWEETS
Sweets may contain gelatine, cochineal and animal fats.

WORCESTERSHIRE SAUCE
Most brands contain anchovies, but vegetarian versions do exist.

YOGURT, CRÈME FRAÎCHE, FROMAGE FRAIS AND ICE CREAM
Some low-fat varieties may contain gelatine.

Source: The Vegetarian Society

TYPES OF VEGETABLE

The mainstays of most vegetarian diets are the colourful, flavourful vegetables that bring variety to every meal. Not only are vegetables packed with vital vitamins and minerals, and lots of dietary fibre, they are versatile ingredients that can be baked, boiled, fried, stir-fried, steamed – and even enjoyed raw. There is no reason for a vegetarian meal to be bland or dull!

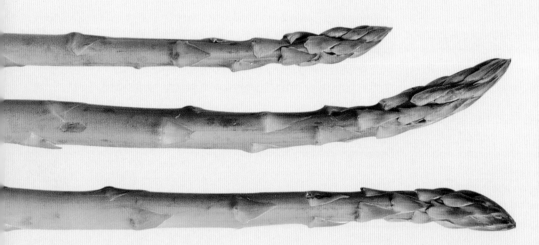

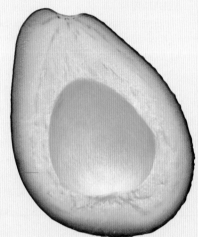

Roots, shoots & stems
Artichokes Asparagus Beansprouts Beetroots Carrots Fennel Potatoes Sweet Potatoes

When it comes to filling soups, stews and roasts, few ingredients beat hearty roots and tubers – but roots also make interesting, colourful salads. As well as containing various nutrients, roots are an excellent source of complex carbohydrate, which provides energy throughout the day. Beansprouts can be used in stir-fries and salads.

Buy dry, firm beetroots, carrots, fennel, potatoes and sweet potatoes. Asparagus and celery should be firm and snap easily and crisply. Beansprouts should be crisp and creamy white in colour, without any brown.

Squashes & fruit
Avocados Aubergines Butternut Squash Courgettes Cucumbers Peppers Pumpkins Tomatoes

The bright and vibrant colours of these vegetables tell you at a glance that they are bursting with goodness. The tomato is actually a fruit, but is treated as a vegetable, and all these ingredients are collectively known as 'vegetable fruits', because they carry the seeds of the plant on which they grow. All vegetable fruits can be baked, boiled, roasted and stir-fried, but avocados, courgettes, peppers and tomatoes also make excellent, healthy salads when eaten raw.

When shopping, look for plump, firm vegetables with unblemished skins. Buy them loose, if possible, rather than packed. Keep them in the fridge for up to a week, except avocados, which should be chilled for a maximum of two days.

The onion family & mushrooms

Garlic Leeks Cultivated and wild mushrooms Onions

Cooks would be lost without these essential ingredients – the many varieties of onions and mushrooms flavour and add aroma and bulk to everything from delicately flavoured cooking stocks to filling baked casseroles. Although garlic and onions have a pungent, full flavour, slow, gentle cooking transforms them to sweet richness. Red onions and spring onions can also be eaten raw.

Cultivated mushrooms are often bland, more valued for their texture than their flavour, but experiment with different wild mushrooms and enjoy their intense flavours when cooked or added raw to salads.

Only buy onions and heads of garlic that feel heavy for their size with dry, papery skins; avoid any sprouting ones. Leeks should be firm with a white bottom and 'fresh' green tops. Spring onions should also be firm, not limp. Spring onions are best kept in the fridge, but leeks will last for up to a week in a cool, dry place.

Brassicas & leaves

Broccoli Brussels sprouts Cabbage Cauliflower Chicory Lettuce Pak Choi Rocket Spinach Watercress

These fresh green vegetables are equally tempting raw in salads or cooked, with rocket and watercress adding a zingy, peppery note. Broccoli, Brussels sprouts, cabbage and cauliflower are members of the vitamin-C-rich brassica family, and contain compounds that are believed to reduce the risk of cancer.

For maximum nutritional value, buy whole heads, rather than broccoli and cauliflower florets, avoiding any brown leaves. Brussels sprouts should have firm, tight leaves, and pak choi should have crisp, not limp, leaves. Look for fresh rocket, spinach and watercress leaves without any wilting; store in the fridge and use within two days of purchase. Mixed salad leaves can be bought in sealed bags, conveniently washed and ready for use, but the washing process often depletes the nutrients. If you grow your own salad leaves, try to pick them early in the morning, for same day use, and store them in a polythene bag in the refrigerator.

TYPES OF FRUIT

Like vegetables, the range of fruit from which to choose is incredibly diverse. It is easy to routinely buy the same types every week, but it really is worth experimenting with new varieties and broadening your culinary repertoire.

The ultimate convenience food, most fruit simply needs a wash and is ready to eat. As most nutrients are found just below the skin, avoid peeling if possible and preferably eat raw rather than cooked, as the cooking process affects nutrient levels. Good quality and freshness are essential when buying fruit; not only will it taste better and last longer, but it will be higher in antioxidant nutrients. Buy organic whenever you can and avoid bulk-buying if the fruit is going to sit in the fruit bowl or refrigerator for days.

Citrus fruit

Vibrantly coloured oranges, lemons, grapefruit, clementines and limes are packed with beneficial vitamin C and beta carotene. They make a versatile addition to the kitchen, lending themselves to both sweet and savoury dishes. Once cut or peeled, use straight away, as vitamin C levels diminish from the moment you slice the fruit.

Orange
Popular varieties of orange include the juicy Jaffa, Valencia and navel (named after the belly-button-type spot at the flower end). Thin-skinned oranges tend to be the juiciest. Marmalade is made from the sour-tasting Seville orange. Orange rind or peel adds a fragrant note to cakes, biscuits and sweet sauces, as well as savoury dishes.

Lemon
Lemons (juice and rind) are an essential ingredient in the kitchen; just a squeeze of juice will add zing to salad dressings, vegetables and marinades. The rind also enlivens both sweet and savoury dishes. Lemon juice can also prevent some fruit and vegetables, such as avocado and apples, discolouring when cut. Avoid those with green patches on the skin, as this is a sign of unripeness.

Lime
Limes have a sharper flavour than lemons and are often used in Indian, Indonesian and Thai cooking, adding a fragrant note.

How to Segment Citrus Fruit

Use a serrated knife to cut off a slice from the top and bottom of the fruit to reveal the flesh. Remove the skin and white pith, either in a spiral, beginning at the cut top and following the curve of the fruit, or by standing the fruit on the cut base and cutting down from top to bottom around the fruit.

Hold the fruit in the palm of your hand over a bowl. Use a small fruit knife to cut in front of the membrane. Push the knife forward to remove the segment cleanly from the membrane. Cut in front of the next membrane, then again push the knife forward towards the outer edge of the fruit – the segment will drop into the bowl.

Continue to separate all the segments from the membrane, then squeeze the membrane tightly. Unless using the segments immediately, put in a small bowl, cover with clingfilm and refrigerate to prevent the air oxidizing the fruit and making it bitter.

Orchard fruit

Probably the most popular group of fruit, ranging from crisp apples to succulent peaches and juicy cherries.

Apple

There are hundreds of different varieties of apple, and many shops are now beginning to stock some of the more unusual types. The Bramley is the most widely used cooking apple, but does require sweetening with sugar. Some eating apples are equally good stewed in a little water and no extra sugar is required.

Peach

Gorgeous succulent peaches range in colour from gold to deep red and the flesh can be golden or white. Nectarines are similar, but without the fuzzy skin. Buy both peaches and nectarines slightly hard and then ripen them at home. They bruise easily, so care is needed when handling.

Pear

Like certain apples, some varieties of pear are good for cooking, while others are best eaten raw. Pears are best in the late summer and autumn with the arrival of the new season's crop. Particular favourites are the plump Comice, green-brown-skinned Conference and yellow-skinned Williams.

Cherry

Glossy, sweet red cherries make a welcome appearance in stores in the summer months. There are two types of cherry: sweet and sour. The latter is best when cooked.

Plum

Plums are a popular summer fruit and vary in colour and flavour from yellow to purple and from the sweet and juicy to the slightly tart. The latter are best cooked in pies and cakes.

Currants

These tiny baubles of brightly coloured fruit make a pretty addition to desserts. Blackcurrants, whitecurrants and redcurrants are usually sold in bunches on the stem. To remove the currants from the stalk, run the prongs of a fork down through the clusters, taking care not to damage the fruit. Currants can be a little on the tart side and may benefit from a sprinkling of sugar. They look attractive in fruit salads, pies and the traditional British summer pudding, or can easily be transformed into jellies and jams.

Berries

Usually at their best in the summer, most berries are now readily available all year round.

Strawberry

Strawberries, if at their peak of ripeness (avoid those with white or green tips), need little embellishment; a spoonful of cream or crème fraîche will suffice. Strawberries contain plenty of vitamin C, and they are a good source of B vitamins.

Raspberry

Raspberries are very fragile and don't have a long shelf life. Their soft, delicate texture and aromatic flavour are best suited to simple preparations.

Gooseberry

Gooseberries are a popular fruit in northern Europe, but are relatively rare in other parts of the world. They range from the tart green variety with the fuzzy skin, which is best suited to pies, crumbles and jams, to the softer, sweeter, purple type. This can be mixed with cream or custard to make a fruit fool.

Blackberry

Blackberries are a familiar sight in British hedgerows in early autumn, but the cultivated type have a longer season. Juicy and plump, blackberries vary in sweetness. Often used in cooking, they are delicious in summer pudding, tarts, pies and crumbles, or puréed to make a sauce that goes with ice cream or nut roasts.

Blueberry

Ripe blueberries are plump and slightly firm, with a natural 'bloom'. They are delicious eaten raw, but can also be made into jams and jellies and baked into pies, tarts, cakes and muffins.

Grapes

Grapes range in colour from deep purple to pale red, and from vibrant green to almost white. Most grapes are grown for wine production; those for eating tend to be less acidic and have a thinner skin. Try to buy organic grapes or wash well before eating. The fruit should be plump and firm, and firmly attached to the stalk.

Melons

When buying melons, look for those that are heavy for their size, yield to gentle pressure and smell fragrant

at the stem end – this is a sign of ripeness. There is a wide range to choose from, including the pinkish-red watermelon, yellow honeydew and orange-fleshed cantaloupe. Watermelons are very low in calories owing to their high water content and make a refreshing summer dessert. Avoid buying them ready-sliced, as vitamin levels will have diminished.

Tropical fruit

This exotic collection of fruit ranges from the popular banana to the more unusual pawpaw (or papaya).

Banana

The high starch content of bananas means that they provide plenty of energy as well as fibre, vitamins and minerals. The soft, creamy flesh can be baked whole, frozen to make a quick ice cream, blended into smoothies or mashed into cakes. Bananas with patches of green can be ripened at room temperature, but it is not advisable to buy entirely green fruit, as they rarely ripen properly.

Pineapple

Pineapples have a sweet and juicy flesh. Choose fruit that are heavy for their size and are slightly tender when pressed, with fresh green spiky leaves. The fruit is ripe when you can successfully pull out a leaf without tugging. Pineapples are particularly good for the digestive system.

Pawpaw

The slightly pear-shaped pawpaw has a speckled yellow skin when ripe, a vibrant pinkish-orange pulp and an incredibly perfumed flavour. The numerous edible seeds taste peppery when dried. Pawpaw is best eaten raw, although unripe green fruit can be used in cooking.

Mango

Mangoes have a wonderfully fragrant, juicy pulp when ripe, which can be used in a wide range of both sweet and savoury dishes, turned into smoothies, ice cream, purées and sauces, and added to salsas and salads. The skin ranges in colour from green to yellow, orange or red. A mango that is entirely green is likely to be unripe, although in Asia these are often sliced into salads.

Kiwi fruit

Kiwi fruit or Chinese gooseberries are particularly rich in vitamin C. The puréed flesh can be used to make refreshing sorbets and ice creams. Slice in half and scoop out the flesh and seeds with a spoon for a healthy snack or use in fruit salads.

Passion fruit

Passion fruit does not look particularly inviting, with its dark wrinkly skin, but inside is a fragrant mixture of golden pulp and edible black seeds.

TYPES OF GRAIN, CEREAL, PULSE & BEAN

When we think of grains, rice, wheat and oats immediately spring to mind, yet this group is surprisingly large and each type comes in various forms, from the whole grain to flour. For most of us, grains form a major part of our diet and a very nutritious one at that: they are not only high in complex carbohydrates, they also contain essential protein, fibre, vitamins and minerals, and are low in fat. Unprocessed types, such as those used in wholemeal bread and pasta, are richer in these nutrients, since the refining process depletes much of the goodness of the grain. Inexpensive and readily available, grains make a versatile addition to the storecupboard.

To ensure freshness, always buy grains and their related products from shops that have a regular turnover of stock. Store in airtight containers in a cool, dry, dark cupboard to prevent them becoming stale and to keep moisture out.

Wheat
The most widely available grain crop in the Western world, wheat comes in various forms.

Storing and Reusing Cooked Rice

Leftover cooked rice can be kept in an airtight container in the refrigerator. Make sure it is thoroughly cooled before refrigerating. If it is being used cold in salads, chill and use within a day. Reheat cooked rice thoroughly. Microwave it until it is piping hot or tip it into a saucepan of boiling water and reheat it for 1 minute only, or steam it over boiling water. If it is not used within two days, cooked rice is susceptible to a bacteria, *Bacillus cereus*, which can cause stomach upsets.

Flour
Flour is ground from the whole grain and may be wholemeal or white, depending on the degree of processing. Strong or hard flour is high in gluten, which makes it ideal for breadmaking, while soft flour is lower in gluten and higher in starch, making it better for cakes and pastries. Durum wheat flour is one of the hardest wheat varieties and is used to make pasta.

Other forms of wheat
Wheat comes in many forms, including wheat berries, bran flakes, cracked wheat, bulgar wheat, semolina, wheat grass and couscous. The latter, which looks like a grain, is actually a form of pasta made by steaming and drying cracked durum wheat.

Rice
Almost every culture in the world has its own culinary repertoire of rice dishes, ranging from Spanish paella to Indian biryani.

Long-grain and brown rice
Long-grain is the most widely used type of rice; brown rice has a nuttier, chewier texture than white, which contains less fibre and fewer nutrients.

Basmati
Basmati, available in both white and brown varieties, is a slender, long-grain rice and is aged for a year after harvest. Widely used in Indian dishes, its light, fluffy grain is also good for rice salads.

Thai and Japanese rice
Thai or jasmine rice has a soft, sticky texture and a mild, perfumed flavour – which explains its other name, fragrant rice. Japanese rice also has a soft, sticky texture and is mixed with rice vinegar to make sushi rolls.

Arborio, Carnaroli and Valencia
Arborio and Carnaroli are classic risotto rices. The short, stubby grain absorbs about five times its weight in water, creating a creamy result. Valencia rice, used for paella, is also a short-grain rice, but it is not quite as starchy as risotto rice.

Other forms of rice
Other forms to look out for are pudding rice, red rice and wild rice; the latter, with its slender black grains, is not in fact a true rice but an aquatic grass.

Other grains
Oats
Like rye, oats are a popular grain in Northern Europe. Flaked and rolled oats are used to make porridge and muesli. Medium and fine oatmeal is best in oatcakes and breads. Oats are believed to reduce cholesterol levels in the blood.

Corn
Also known as maize, corn comes in yellow, blue, red and even black varieties. We are most familiar with yellow corn, which is used for cornmeal or polenta, cornflour and popcorn.

Rye
Rye flour is commonly used to make a dark, dense bread, particularly in Eastern Europe, Scandinavia and Russia. The strong-tasting grain can also be used in savoury dishes.

Quinoa
This highly nutritious grain is one of the few plant foods that is a complete protein, which means it contains all eight essential amino acids. The tiny bead-like grain has a mild, slightly bitter taste and can be used to make tabbouleh, stuffings, bakes, pilafs and breakfast cereals.

Millet
This grain is not widely used, but it is highly nutritious, containing more iron than most other grains, and is a good source of zinc. The tiny bead-like grains have a mild flavour and make the perfect accompaniment to stews and curries, and can be used in pilafs, tabbouleh, milk puddings and porridge. Millet is also gluten-free.

Barley
Pearl barley is the most common form and is husked, steamed and polished to give it its characteristic ivory-coloured look. Pot barley is the whole grain and takes much longer to cook than pearl. Both types make a satisfying porridge and can be added to stews, bakes and soups.

TYPES OF DAIRY PRODUCE

Dairy produce provides vegetarians with valuable protein as well as calcium and vitamins D and B, including B12. Many dairy products are naturally high in fat and should therefore be eaten sparingly, or, alternatively, you could replace them with reduced-fat alternatives. For those who do not eat dairy products, there is an increasing number of dairy-free substitutes to choose from, many of which have culinary properties similar to their dairy counterparts

Milk, cream and yogurt

Milk
Cow's milk is one of our most widely used ingredients. Skimmed and semi-skimmed versions now outsell their full-fat counterpart, but they are not nutritionally inferior. Organic milk is now widely available, and comes from cows that have been fed a pesticide-free diet and are not routinely treated with hormones. For those who are intolerant of cow's milk, there are varieties of goat's and sheep's milk, which are nutritionally similar, but easier to digest.

Cream
The fat content of cream varies enormously, ranging from about 12 per cent for half-fat through to a decadent 55 per cent for clotted cream. Crème fraîche is a rich, cultured cream with a fat content of around 35 per cent, but it now comes in low-fat versions (around 10 per cent). A spoonful adds a delicious creaminess to sauces and it is also excellent dolloped on to fresh fruit, especially strawberries. Soured cream is treated with lactic acid, which gives it its characteristic tang. It contains 20 per cent fat, although it is possible to buy reduced-fat versions. If using in cooking, take care that it does not curdle.

Yogurt
The fat content of yogurt ranges from 0.5 per cent through to 10 per cent for thick Greek-style yogurt. Although the latter is higher in fat than most types of yogurt, it is lower in fat than cream and makes a useful replacement in cooking, as it does not curdle, unlike low-fat varieties. Live or bio-yogurts have been fermented with beneficial bacteria that can aid digestion and have a mild, creamy flavour.

Non-Dairy Alternatives

It is important for vegans in particular to ensure their diet includes the protein, minerals and vitamins found in dairy products. The best source is the soya bean. Tofu, or soya cheese, made from cooked soya beans, is an excellent non-meat protein that is cholesterol free. As well as being a useful source of calcium, tofu also contains vitamin E, manganese, phosphorus and iron. Milk, cream and yogurt products are also made from dried soya beans. Other products that are nutritionally similar to cow's milk are milk and cheese substitutes made from oats, rice and nuts. Pure vegetable margarines and spreads are also available.

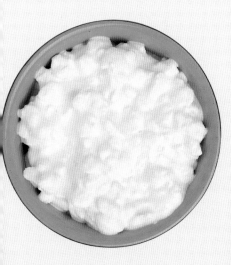

Fresh unripened cheeses

Young, immature cheeses are unlikely to contain rennet and have a light, mild flavour.

Cottage cheese
Cottage cheese is one of the most popular and is lower in fat – 2–5 per cent – than most other cheeses. Cottage cheese is a soft, fresh-curd variety of cheese and is available in large- and small-curd varieties.

Fromage frais
Fromage frais is a smooth, fresh cheese with the same consistency as thick yogurt, but is less acidic. The fat content varies from almost nothing to about 8 per cent. It can be used in much the same way as yogurt.

Italian ricotta
Italian ricotta can be made from sheep's or cow's milk and has a slightly granular texture. Its mild, clean flavour means that it can be used in both savoury and sweet dishes.

Cream cheese and Quark
Cream cheese has a rich, velvety consistency, while Quark is a low-fat curd cheese. Both are perfect for making cheesecakes, dips and spreads.

Fresh ripened cheeses
Brie and Camembert
These fresh, soft, cow's milk cheeses originally came from France. When fully ripe, they have an invitingly buttery texture that 'oozes' inside. Camembert tends to have a stronger flavour than Brie, which is enhanced when served at room temperature.

Other soft and hard cheeses
The following gives just a taster of other soft and hard cheeses that are all readily available in vegetarian rennet versions.

Mozzarella
Mozzarella has a delicate, silky texture, as well as excellent melting properties, hence its use on pizzas and bakes. It is usually made from cow's milk, but the traditional cheese is made from buffalo's milk and is called mozzarella di bufala.

Halloumi
Halloumi has been called the vegetarian alternative to bacon. It has a firm, rubbery texture and salty flavour; cut it into slices and grill or griddle.

Feta
Feta can be soaked in water for 10 minutes to remove its saltiness. It has a firm, crumbly texture and is used in the classic Greek salad. It was once made with goat's or sheep's milk, but is now more often made with cow's milk.

Cheddar
Cheddar is a national favourite, but it varies tremendously in quality. Look for mature or vintage traditional farmhouse Cheddar, which is aged for between nine and 24 months and has a rich, almost nutty flavour.

HERBS AND SPICES

Highly regarded for thousands of years, herbs and spices can enliven even the simplest of dishes. Invaluable ingredients in the vegetarian kitchen, they enhance the aroma and flavour of both savoury and sweet dishes. They also have a positive effect on the digestive system. Although the directory of herbs below concentrates on fresh herbs, dried herbs provide a useful alternative, especially during the winter months when some fresh herbs are not available.

Herbs

Fresh herbs are now sold loose, in pots or packets. It is possible to increase the shelf life of the latter by removing the herbs from the packet and immersing the stems in a jar of water. Cover with a polythene bag, then seal with an elastic band; the herbs should keep for up to a week.

Basil
Basil is a popular fresh herb and is commonly used in Italian dishes, especially pesto. The purple variety is widely used in Thai cooking. The fragile leaves are best torn rather than cut with a knife to prevent them bruising. Drying basil impairs its taste and so is not recommended.

Coriander
Another favourite in Thai cooking, the warm and spicy flavour of coriander also enlivens Indian dishes. The root is edible and can be ground into Indian and Thai curry pastes.

Mint
There are numerous varieties of mint, with peppermint and spearmint being the most readily available. Mint can be mixed with natural yogurt to make raita, a calming accompaniment to hot curries; immersed in hot water to make a refreshing mint tea; or used in the fragrant salad, tabbouleh.

Dill
Dill is a scented herb. The feather-like leaves of the plant are used as a herb, while the seeds come from the flower heads after they have matured.

Tarragon
Tarragon is popular in French cooking and has a great affinity with egg and cheese dishes.

Chives
Chives are a part of the onion family, but have a milder flavour that works best when sprinkled over salads, eggs and tomato-based dishes as a garnish.

Bay
The attractive, glossy green leaves of the bay tree add a robust, spicy flavour to stocks and stews, and are used in bouquet garni. The leaf is used whole and is usually removed before the end of cooking as it is not readily digestible.

Oregano
Oregano is one of the few fresh herbs that dry well. Closely related to marjoram, but with a more robust flavour, oregano especially complements tomato-based dishes. Both oregano and thyme work well in marinades and are largely interchangeable in their uses.

Parsley
Both flat-leaf and curly-leaf parsley are commonly available. Flat-leaf parsley looks similar to coriander and is preferable to the curly type for use in cooking.

Sage, rosemary and thyme
Sage is pungent in flavour, but works well with nut roasts, bakes and stews. Rosemary has a strong, aromatic flavour and works best in hearty soups and stews whose flavours will not be overwhelmed. Thyme has a strong piquant or lemony flavour.

Spices

Spices – the seeds, fruit, pods, bark and buds of plants – should be bought in small quantities from a shop with a regular turnover of stock. Aroma is the best indication of freshness, as this diminishes when a spice is stale. Store spices in airtight jars away from direct sunlight.

Ginger
Ginger has a warming, slightly peppery flavour that is different from the fresh root. It is used to flavour cakes, breads and biscuits, and added to curries, stews and soups.

Cardamom
Pungent, warm and aromatic, the spice known as cardamom is derived from several plants. It is sold as a seed pod or ground as a spice.

Cumin and coriander
A key component in Middle Eastern, North African and Indian cooking, cumin comes both ground and in whole seed form. Black seeds, also known as nigella, have a sweeter and milder flavour than the brown seeds. Ground coriander is used in much the same way as cumin, while the ivory-coloured whole seeds are often used as a pickling spice as well as ground in curries and tagines.

Cinnamon, nutmeg and cloves
These have a wonderfully warming flavour and are often used together in cakes, puddings and biscuits. Whole cinnamon sticks (quills) are used to flavour curries, pilafs and fruit compotes.

Saffron
Saffron is the world's most expensive spice. Made from the dried stigmas of *Crocus sativus*, only a tiny amount is required to add a distinctive flavour and a golden colour to paella, stews and milky puddings.

Pepper
Pepper is undoubtedly the most widely used spice and comes in a multitude of colours – black, white, pink and green. The spice adds its own flavour to dishes and brings out the flavour of other ingredients.

Cayenne and paprika
Cayenne is a fiery spice that adds colour and flavour to curries, soups and stews. Paprika is milder and can be used more liberally. Both are said to be good for the circulation.

Vanilla
Vanilla pods provide a fragrant, mellow, sweet taste, with a rich, perfumed aroma. They are often used in sweet dishes.

How to Freeze Herbs

Herbs must be in perfect condition before they are frozen: anything stale, bruised or contaminated will not be improved by freezing.

Wash the herbs carefully and shake dry. Lay out on kitchen paper to dry completely, then transfer to a tray and open freeze in a single layer. Once frozen, pack into small bags or boxes and use as required. Alternatively, chop the washed and dried herbs (they will bruise and blacken if they are not dry) and pack into ice-cube trays to half fill. Top up with water and freeze. Drop the herb ice cubes into stews, soups and casseroles for an instant herb seasoning.

ESSENTIAL COOKING TECHNIQUES

While most vegetables can be eaten raw, there are numerous cooking techniques that will add interest and variety to vegetarian meals. You can maximize the flavour, colour and texture of the vegetables, while preserving as much of the essential vitamins and nutrients as possible. Since vegetables are so central to your diet, it's well worth your while considering how best to cook them.

Boiling

The traditional method of cooking vegetables is to use plenty of salted water and a large, uncovered saucepan. This method is most suitable for sweetcorn, potatoes and other root vegetables. Although steaming is preferable when cooking green vegetables because they retain more nutrients, if you choose to boil them leave them uncovered; put the lid on and they lose their attractive bright green colour. Choose an appropriate size of saucepan for the quantity of vegetables so that the water can circulate, but use the minimum amount of water, cook for the briefest period and drain the vegetables immediately, because boiling destroys water-soluble vitamins, such as B and C. Other soluble nutrients leach into the cooking water, so get into the habit of keeping the cooking water and using it as a base for soup or sauces.

Freshly Prepared...

The fresher the ingredients, the higher their nutrient content. Avoid old, tired, wilted vegetables and do not store anything for long at home. It is far better to buy fresh and loose when you need them, and to select organic if you can, in preference to ready-prepared packs, which will have lost some of their vitamins as well as their flavour. If possible, avoid peeling vegetables, because many nutrients are stored close to or in the skin (or put the peelings into a pot to make stock). Wash or scrub everything, but don't leave vegetables soaking in water or their soluble nutrients will leach out. Similarly, do not cut or prepare vegetables too far in advance, as some vitamins, such as vitamin C, diminish once the cut surface is exposed to the air.

Poaching

A less vigorous way to cook more delicate vegetables is to put them in boiling liquid (water, stock, wine or milk), then to simmer them gently over a low heat to retain their flavour, texture and shape.

Frying

Deep-frying is less popular these days, with concerns over the amount of fat in our diet. In fact, if the cooking temperature is correct, deep-fried foods are quickly sealed and absorb less oil than when they are shallow-fried. Coating vegetables in batter or in egg and breadcrumbs forms a crispy seal, which also reduces oil absorption. Deep-frying is a long-established cooking method for potatoes (chips) and also works well for aubergines and courgettes. Dry-frying in a frying pan or griddle pan or on a flat griddle plate is a healthier option that can be used for some vegetables as well as for halloumi cheese.

Steaming

Less water comes into contact with vegetables when they are steamed rather than boiled, so they are crisper and retain more essential nutrients. Also, some vegetables – mangetout, leeks and courgettes – become limp and unappetizing if boiled. Steamed new potatoes are particularly delicious; try putting some fresh mint leaves under the potatoes to flavour them while they are steaming.

Braising

This cooking method requires only a very little water, and the saucepan is covered. The heat is much reduced and the cooking time greatly increased. You can start by browning the ingredients in a little oil or butter,

Cooking Times

For maximum nutritional benefit, it makes sense to cook your vegetables for the least time possible. Cut them the same size so that they look attractive and cook evenly. While potatoes have to be cooked right through, other root vegetables, such as carrots, are best served with a little 'bite' to them. Boil for less time or steam your vegetables and enjoy the extra crunch. Some vegetables – those with a high water content such as spinach, celery or beansprouts – need only be blanched in boiling water for 30 seconds. For frying or stir-frying, ensure that the oil is properly hot before adding the vegetables. When time is short, try microwaving your vegetables. This method requires less liquid or fat as well as shorter cooking times than conventional cooking.

then add water or other liquid before covering the saucepan. The small amount of liquid that remains at the end of cooking will be sweet and flavoured – serve the vegetables with this juice and you gain all the nutrients. Onions, turnips, leeks, chicory, celery and fennel lend themselves to braising. Red cabbage is one of the brassicas that positively benefits from this long, slow method of cooking.

Stir-frying

This method of frying in a little oil over a very high heat has become widely popular. Stir-fried vegetables retain far more of their nutritional value, flavour, texture and colour. They are very thinly sliced and rapidly moved around in a hot wok to aid fast and even cooking. Most of us are familiar with stir-fried baby sweetcorn, mangetout, peppers, beansprouts and bamboo shoots, but the method is an equally good way to cook thinly sliced cauliflower, Brussels sprouts, cabbage and carrots.

Roasting

Traditionally, roasting vegetables meant cooking them in the fat dripping from a joint of meat. The far healthier vegetarian option is to roast vegetables that have been lightly drizzled with olive oil in a roasting tin, to which you can add garlic and herbs for additional flavour. Squash, parsnips, potatoes, peppers, onions, tomatoes, asparagus and even beetroots are all delicious cooked in this way; their flavour is concentrated and the natural sweetness of the vegetables is accentuated.

Sautéeing and sweating

These methods use less oil than traditional shallow-frying and are longer, slower processes than stir-frying. Sautéeing is done in an uncovered frying pan; sweating in either a heavy-based lidded casserole or frying pan – water evaporating from the ingredients is trapped and falls back into the pan. Onions are often sweated to soften them without colouring.

Baking

Potatoes, onions and garlic can be baked 'dry' in their skins, while softer vegetables (peppers and tomatoes) can be stuffed with rice and other fillings or wrapped in foil.

Grilling and barbecuing

The intense heat from a grill or barbecue is unsuitable for either delicate or dense vegetables, which become charred rather than cooked, but excellent for softer ones, such as onions, sweetcorn, peppers, aubergines and tomatoes. All vegetables need to be brushed with oil before being placed on the grill.

BASIC RECIPES

The recipes in this book provide a wide variety of delicious vegetarian meals. Some of them incorporate a common basic recipe, to which you can refer on these pages, or you can use these basic recipes as an addition to a dish of your choice.

VEGETABLE STOCK
MAKES: 2 LITRES/3½ PINTS

- 2 TBSP SUNFLOWER OR CORN OIL
- 115 G/4 OZ ONIONS, FINELY CHOPPED
- 115 G/4 OZ LEEKS, FINELY CHOPPED
- 115 G/4 OZ CARROTS, FINELY CHOPPED
- 4 CELERY STICKS, FINELY CHOPPED
- 85 G/3 OZ FENNEL, FINELY CHOPPED
- 85 G/3 OZ TOMATOES, FINELY CHOPPED
- 2.25 LITRES/4 PINTS WATER
- 1 BOUQUET GARNI

Heat the oil in a large saucepan over a low heat. Add the onions and leeks and cook, stirring frequently, for 5 minutes, or until soft.
Add the remaining vegetables, cover and cook over a very low heat, stirring occasionally, for 10 minutes. Add the water and bouquet garni and bring to the boil, then reduce the heat and simmer for 20 minutes.
Strain, leave to cool, then cover and store in the refrigerator. Use within 3 days or freeze in portions for up to 3 months.

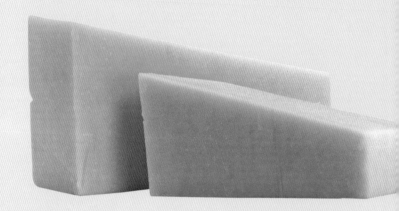

CHEESE SAUCE
MAKES: 600 ML/1 PINT

- 40 G/1½ OZ BUTTER
- 5 TBSP PLAIN FLOUR
- 600 ML/1 PINT MILK
- 140 G/5 OZ CHEDDAR CHEESE, GRATED
- SALT AND PEPPER

Melt the butter in a saucepan over a medium heat. Stir in the flour and cook, stirring constantly, for 1–2 minutes. Remove from the heat and gradually whisk in the milk. Return to the heat and bring to the boil, whisking constantly. Simmer for 2 minutes, or until the sauce is thick and glossy. Remove from the heat, add the cheese and stir until melted. Season to taste with salt and pepper.

TOMATO SAUCE
MAKES: 150 ML/5 FL OZ

- 1 TBSP OLIVE OIL
- 1 SMALL ONION, CHOPPED
- 1 GARLIC CLOVE, CHOPPED
- 400 G/14 OZ CANNED CHOPPED
  TOMATOES
- 2 TBSP CHOPPED FRESH PARSLEY
- 1 TSP DRIED OREGANO
- 2 BAY LEAVES
- 2 TBSP TOMATO PURÉE
- 1 TSP SUGAR
- SALT AND PEPPER

Heat the oil in a saucepan over a medium heat. Add the onion and cook, stirring, for 2–3 minutes until beginning to soften.
Add the garlic and cook, stirring, for 1 minute. Stir in the tomatoes, parsley, oregano, bay leaves, tomato purée and sugar and season to taste with salt and pepper.
Bring the sauce to the boil, then reduce the heat and simmer, uncovered, for 15–20 minutes until the sauce has reduced by half. Remove and discard the bay leaves just before serving.

PESTO SAUCE
MAKES: 75 ML/2½ FL OZ

- 55 G/2 OZ FRESH BASIL
  LEAVES
- 15 G/½ OZ PINE KERNELS
- 1 GARLIC CLOVE
- PINCH OF SALT
- 25 G/1 OZ PARMESAN CHEESE, FRESHLY GRATED
- 3 TBSP EXTRA VIRGIN OLIVE OIL

Put the basil leaves, pine kernels, garlic and salt in a mortar and pound to a paste with a pestle.
Transfer to a bowl and, with a wooden spoon, gradually work in the Parmesan cheese, followed by the oil, to make a thick, creamy sauce.
Cover with clingfilm and refrigerate until required.

MAYONNAISE
MAKES: 300 ML/10 FL OZ

- 2 EGG YOLKS
- 150 ML/5 FL OZ SUNFLOWER OIL
- 150 ML/5 FL OZ OLIVE OIL
- 1 TBSP WHITE WINE VINEGAR
- 2 TSP DIJON MUSTARD
- SALT AND PEPPER

Beat the egg yolks with a pinch of salt in a bowl.
Whisk the oils together in a jug. Gradually add one quarter of the oil mixture to the egg yolks, a drop at a time, beating constantly with a whisk or electric mixer.
Beat in the vinegar, then continue adding the oils in a steady stream, beating constantly.
Once all the oil has been incorporated, stir in the mustard and season to taste with salt and pepper.

TZATZIKI
MAKES: 500 ML/18 FL OZ

- 500 ML/18 FL OZ NATURAL GREEK-STYLE YOGURT OR OTHER THICK NATURAL YOGURT
- 4 GARLIC CLOVES, VERY FINELY CHOPPED
- 2 CUCUMBERS, PEELED, DESEEDED AND VERY FINELY DICED
- 1 TBSP LEMON-FLAVOURED OR EXTRA VIRGIN OLIVE OIL
- 3 TBSP LEMON JUICE
- 1 TBSP CHOPPED FRESH MINT LEAVES
- SALT AND PEPPER
- PAPRIKA, TO GARNISH

TO SERVE
- CELERY BATONS
- CARROT BATONS
- PITTA BREAD TRIANGLES

Put the yogurt, garlic, cucumber, oil, lemon juice and mint in a serving bowl and stir together until well combined. Season to taste with salt and pepper, cover with clingfilm and chill in the refrigerator for at least 2 hours, or until required.

When ready to use, garnish with a little paprika. Serve with the celery and carrot batons and the pitta bread triangles for dipping.

RICH SHORTCRUST PASTRY
MAKES: 1 X 23-CM/9-INCH FLAN

- 175 G/6 OZ PLAIN FLOUR
- PINCH OF SALT
- 85 G/3 OZ BUTTER, DICED, PLUS EXTRA FOR GREASING
- 1 EGG YOLK
- 3 TBSP ICE-COLD WATER

Sift the flour with the salt into a bowl. Add the butter and rub into the flour with your fingertips until the mixture resembles fine breadcrumbs.

Beat the egg yolk with the water in a small bowl. Sprinkle the liquid over the flour mixture and combine with a round-bladed knife or your fingertips to form a dough. Shape the dough into a ball, wrap in foil and chill in the refrigerator for 30 minutes.

PIZZA DOUGH BASES

MAKES: 2 X 25-CM/10-INCH PIZZAS

- 225 G/8 OZ PLAIN FLOUR, PLUS EXTRA FOR DUSTING
- 1 TSP SALT
- 6 TBSP LUKEWARM WATER
- 2 TBSP OLIVE OIL, PLUS EXTRA FOR OILING
- 1 TSP EASY-BLEND DRIED YEAST

Sift the flour with the salt into a large, warmed bowl and make a well in the centre. Add the water, oil and yeast to the well. Using a wooden spoon or your hands, gradually mix in, drawing the flour from the sides, to form a dough. Turn out on to a lightly floured work surface and knead for 5 minutes, or until smooth and elastic. Form the dough into a ball, put in a clean, lightly oiled bowl and cover with oiled clingfilm. Leave in a warm place to rise for 1 hour, or until doubled in size.

Turn out the dough on to a lightly floured work surface and knock back. Knead briefly before shaping into 2 pizza bases.

PUFF PASTRY

MAKES: 1 X 25-CM/10-INCH FLAN OR PIE

- 175 G/6 OZ PLAIN FLOUR, PLUS EXTRA FOR DUSTING
- PINCH OF SALT
- 175 G/6 OZ UNSALTED BUTTER
- ABOUT 150 ML/5 FL OZ ICE-COLD WATER

Sift the flour with the salt into a large bowl. Dice 25 g/ 1 oz of the butter and rub into the flour with your fingertips. Gradually add the water, just enough to bring the mixture together, and knead briefly to form a smooth dough. Wrap the dough in foil and chill in the refrigerator for 30 minutes. Keep the remaining butter out of the refrigerator, wrap in foil and shape into a 3-cm/1¼-inch thick rectangle. Roll out the dough on a lightly floured work surface to a rectangle 3 times longer and 3 cm/1¼ inches wider than the butter, unwrap the butter and place in the centre of the dough, long side towards you. Fold over the 2 'wings' of pastry to enclose the butter, press down the edges with the rolling pin to seal and then turn the pastry so that the short side is facing you. Roll out the pastry to its original length, fold in 3, turn and roll again to its original length.

Repeat this once more, then rewrap the pastry and chill again for 30 minutes. Repeat the rolling and turning twice more. Chill again for 30 minutes. At this point you can freeze the pastry until you need it.

SHOOTS, ROOTS & STEMS

This chapter will give you new ideas for preparing some of the most familiar, everyday vegetables – Baked Celery with Cream, for example, will stop you from ever again thinking of celery as simply a low-cal salad ingredient. Even the humble potato can take centre stage with recipes such as Roasted Potato Wedges with Shallots & Rosemary and Caramelized Sweet Potatoes. And, for something lighter, try the stir-fried and beansprout salad ideas.

DIRECTORY OF SHOOTS, ROOTS & STEMS

Roots include carrots, potatoes, turnips, celeriac and swedes, comforting and wholesome vegetables that have always been good winter standbys when little else was available. The large group of shoots and stems now available to us offers a wide variety of flavours, ranging from delicately nutty asparagus to bitter chicory and sweet aromatic fennel.

Shoot & stem vegetables

This diverse group includes asparagus, fennel, chicory, celery and the globe artichoke. The distinguished globe artichoke has an exquisite flavour and is great fun to eat: simply boil in water, then dip each leaf into garlic butter, mayonnaise or a vinaigrette dressing. The tastiest part is the heart, which is to be found in the centre of the vegetable, beneath the hairy choke.

Asparagus
There are two types of asparagus: white is picked just before the sprouts reach the surface of the soil, while green-tipped is cut above the ground and develops its colour when it comes into contact with sunlight. Before briefly steaming, boiling, griddling or roasting, trim off the woody end.

Celery
Celery lends a crunchy texture to salads and also makes a good base for soups and stews. Green celery is available all year round, and white is available in winter. Choose stems that are very firm and rigid, but don't forget the leaves, which have a tangy flavour and can be added to stocks. Celery hearts can also be braised.

Chicory
The long, tightly packed leaves of red or white chicory have a distinctive, bitter taste, so use sparingly. Trim the root, remove the core and slice thinly. Chicory can be served raw in salads, steamed or braised.

Fennel
Fennel has a mild aniseed flavour, which is most potent when eaten raw. Roasting fennel (cut into wedges) tempers the flavour and adds a delicious sweetness. Fennel also goes well with many traditional Mediterranean flavours such as tomatoes, olive oil, garlic and basil.

Root vegetables

The comfort foods of the vegetable world, potatoes, carrots, swedes, celeriac, beetroot and parsnips, among others, have a sweet, dense flesh that provides a range of vitamins and minerals, not forgetting fibre.

Potatoes

There are hundreds of different potato varieties and many lend themselves to particular cooking methods. Waxy potatoes, such as Charlotte, are best boiled, or roasted whole, while floury varieties, such as Maris Piper, lend themselves to roasting, baking and mashing. Stored in a dark, well-ventilated place, potatoes will keep for about two weeks. Discard any that develop a green tinge. Sweet potatoes have an orange or white flesh (the former is richer in beta carotene). When cooked, the white-fleshed variety has a drier texture, but both are good roasted, mashed or baked.

Carrots and beetroots

When buying carrots and beetroots, remember that the smaller ones are sweeter. Raw carrots and beetroot can be grated into salads or used to make relishes. Roasting them intensifies their sweetness and both work well in soups.

Celeriac

Celeriac is a knobbly root with a flavour reminiscent of celery. Peel and grate raw into salads, steam, bake or combine with potatoes to make a delicious mash.

Jerusalem artichokes

These small, knobbly tubers have a mild, nutty flavour and are delicious roasted or transformed into soup. Scrub rather than peel before use.

SWEET POTATO & APPLE SOUP

SERVES 6

INGREDIENTS

- 1 TBSP BUTTER
- 3 LEEKS, THINLY SLICED
- 1 LARGE CARROT, THINLY SLICED
- 600 G/1 LB 5 OZ SWEET POTATOES, PEELED AND DICED
- 2 LARGE BRAMLEY APPLES, PEELED AND DICED
- 1.2 LITRES/2 PINTS WATER
- FRESHLY GRATED NUTMEG
- 225 ML/8 FL OZ APPLE JUICE
- 225 ML/8 FL OZ SINGLE CREAM
- SALT AND PEPPER
- SNIPPED FRESH CHIVES OR CORIANDER, TO GARNISH

1 Melt the butter in a large saucepan over a medium–low heat. Add the leeks, cover and cook for 6–8 minutes, or until soft, stirring frequently.

2 Add the carrot, sweet potatoes, apples and water. Season lightly with salt, pepper and nutmeg to taste. Bring to the boil, reduce the heat and simmer, covered, for about 20 minutes, stirring occasionally, until the vegetables are very tender.

3 Allow the soup to cool slightly, then transfer to a blender or food processor and purée until smooth, working in batches if necessary. (If using a food processor, strain off the cooking liquid and reserve. Purée the soup solids with enough cooking liquid to moisten them, then combine with the remaining liquid.)

4 Return the puréed soup to the saucepan and stir in the apple juice. Place over a low heat and simmer for about 10 minutes, until heated through.

5 Stir in the cream and continue simmering for about 5 minutes, stirring frequently, until heated through. Taste and adjust the seasoning, adding more salt, pepper and nutmeg, if necessary. Ladle the soup into warmed bowls, garnish with chives or coriander and serve.

BEETROOT SALAD

SERVES 4–6

INGREDIENTS

- 900 G/2 LB RAW BEETROOTS
- 4 TBSP EXTRA VIRGIN OLIVE OIL
- 1½ TBSP RED WINE VINEGAR
- 2 GARLIC CLOVES, FINELY CHOPPED
- 2 SPRING ONIONS, VERY FINELY CHOPPED
- COARSE SEA SALT

1 Carefully remove the roots from the beetroots without cutting into the skin, then cut off all but 2.5 cm/1 inch of the stalks. Gently rub the beetroots under cold running water, without splitting the skins, to remove any dirt.

2 Put the beetroots in a saucepan with water to cover and bring to the boil. Cover, reduce the heat slightly and cook for 25–40 minutes, depending on the size, until the largest beetroot is tender when you pierce it with a long metal skewer or knife.

3 Meanwhile, put the oil, vinegar, garlic, spring onions and salt to taste in a jar with a screw-top lid and shake until emulsified, then set aside.

4 Drain the beetroots and rinse under cold running water until cool enough to handle, then peel away the skins. Thickly chop or slice the beetroots, then put in a bowl and pour over the dressing. Cover and chill in the refrigerator for at least 1 hour.

5 To serve, gently toss the salad, transfer to a serving platter and serve.

POTATO FRITTERS WITH ONION & TOMATO RELISH

SERVES 8

INGREDIENTS

- 55 G/2 OZ WHOLEMEAL FLOUR
- ½ TSP GROUND CORIANDER
- ½ TSP CUMIN SEEDS
- ¼ TSP CHILLI POWDER
- ½ TSP TURMERIC
- ¼ TSP SALT
- 1 EGG
- 3 TBSP MILK
- 350 G/12 OZ POTATOES, PEELED
- 1–2 GARLIC CLOVES, CRUSHED
- 4 SPRING ONIONS, CHOPPED
- 55 G/2 OZ SWEETCORN KERNELS
- VEGETABLE OIL, FOR SHALLOW FRYING

ONION & TOMATO RELISH

- 1 ONION, PEELED
- 225 G/8 OZ TOMATOES
- 2 TBSP CHOPPED FRESH CORIANDER
- 2 TBSP CHOPPED FRESH MINT
- 2 TBSP LEMON JUICE
- ½ TSP ROASTED CUMIN SEEDS
- ¼ TSP SALT
- PINCH OF CAYENNE PEPPER

1 First make the relish. Cut the onion and tomatoes into small dice and place in a bowl with the remaining ingredients. Mix together well and leave to stand for at least 15 minutes before serving to allow the flavours to blend.

2 Place the flour in a bowl, stir in the spices and salt and make a well in the centre. Add the egg and milk and mix to form a fairly thick batter.

3 Coarsely grate the potatoes, place them in a sieve and rinse well under cold running water. Drain and squeeze dry, then stir them into the batter with the garlic, spring onions and sweetcorn and mix to combine thoroughly.

4 Heat about 5 mm/¼ inch of vegetable oil in a large frying pan and add a few tablespoons of the mixture at a time, flattening each one to form a thin cake. Fry over a low heat, turning frequently, for 2–3 minutes, or until golden brown and cooked through.

5 Drain the fritters on absorbent kitchen paper and keep them hot while frying the remaining mixture in the same way. Serve the potato fritters hot with the Onion & Tomato Relish.

ARTICHOKE & PIMIENTO FLATBREAD

MAKES 12 SLICES

INGREDIENTS

- 4 TBSP SPANISH OLIVE OIL, PLUS EXTRA FOR OILING
- 2 LARGE ONIONS, THINLY SLICED
- 2 GARLIC CLOVES, FINELY CHOPPED
- 400 G/14 OZ CANNED ARTICHOKE HEARTS, DRAINED AND QUARTERED
- 320 G/11¼ OZ BOTTLED OR CANNED PIMIENTOS DEL PIQUILLO, DRAINED AND THINLY SLICED
- 40 G/1½ OZ STONED BLACK SPANISH OLIVES (OPTIONAL)
- SALT AND PEPPER

BREAD DOUGH

- 400 G/14 OZ STRONG WHITE FLOUR, PLUS EXTRA FOR DUSTING
- 1½ TSP EASY-BLEND DRIED YEAST
- 1 TSP SALT
- ½ TSP CASTER SUGAR
- 175 ML/6 FL OZ WARM WATER
- 3 TBSP SPANISH OLIVE OIL

1 To make the bread dough, put the flour, yeast, salt and sugar in a large bowl and make a well in the centre. Mix the water and oil together in a jug, pour into the well and gradually mix in the flour from the sides. Using your hands, mix together to form a soft dough that leaves the sides of the bowl clean.

2 Turn out the dough on to a lightly floured work surface and knead for 10 minutes, or until smooth and elastic and no longer sticky. Shape the dough into a ball and put in a clean bowl. Cover with a clean, damp tea towel and leave in a warm place for 1 hour, or until the dough has risen and doubled in size.

3 Meanwhile, heat 3 tablespoons of the oil in a large frying pan, add the onions and cook over a medium heat, stirring occasionally, for 10 minutes, or until golden brown. Add the garlic and cook, stirring, for 30 seconds until soft. Leave to cool. When cool, stir in the artichoke hearts and pimientos del piquillo, then season to taste with salt and pepper.

4 Preheat the oven to 200°C/400°F/Gas Mark 6. Oil a large baking sheet. Turn out the risen dough on to a lightly floured surface and knead lightly for 2–3 minutes to knock out the air. Roll out the dough to a 30-cm/12-inch square and transfer to the prepared baking sheet.

5 Brush the remaining oil over the dough and spread the artichoke and pimiento mixture on top. Sprinkle over the olives, if using. Bake in the preheated oven for 20–25 minutes until golden brown and crisp. Cut into 12 slices and serve hot or warm.

POTATO GNOCCHI WITH
WALNUT PESTO

SERVES 4

INGREDIENTS
- 450 G/1 LB FLOURY POTATOES
- 55 G/2 OZ PARMESAN CHEESE, FRESHLY GRATED
- 1 EGG, BEATEN
- 200 G/7 OZ PLAIN FLOUR, PLUS EXTRA FOR DUSTING
- SALT AND PEPPER

WALNUT PESTO
- 40 G/1½ OZ FRESH FLAT-LEAF PARSLEY
- 2 TBSP CAPERS, RINSED
- 2 GARLIC CLOVES
- 175 ML/6 FL OZ EXTRA VIRGIN OLIVE OIL
- 70 G/2½ OZ WALNUT HALVES
- 40 G/1½ OZ PECORINO OR PARMESAN CHEESE, FRESHLY GRATED

1 Boil the potatoes in their skins in a large saucepan of water for 30–35 minutes until tender. Drain well and leave to cool slightly.

2 Meanwhile, to make the Walnut Pesto, chop the parsley, capers and garlic, then put in a mortar with the oil, walnuts, and salt and pepper to taste. Pound to a coarse paste in a mortar with a pestle. Add the pecorino cheese and stir well.

3 When the potatoes are cool enough to handle, peel off the skins and pass the flesh through a sieve into a large bowl or press through a potato ricer. While still hot, season well with salt and pepper and add the Parmesan cheese. Beat in the egg and sift in the flour. Lightly mix together, then turn out on to a lightly floured work surface. Knead lightly until the mixture becomes a smooth dough. If it is too sticky, add a little more flour.

4 Using your hands, roll out the dough on a lightly floured work surface into a long log. Cut into 2.5-cm/1-inch pieces and gently press with a fork to give the traditional ridged effect. Transfer to a floured baking sheet and cover with a clean tea towel while you make the remaining gnocchi.

5 Bring a large saucepan of water to the boil, add the gnocchi, in small batches, and cook for 1–2 minutes. Remove with a slotted spoon and transfer to a warmed serving dish to keep warm while you cook the remaining gnocchi.

6 Serve the gnocchi in warmed serving bowls with a good spoonful of the Walnut Pesto on top.

CARROT & ORANGE STIR-FRY

SERVES 4

INGREDIENTS

- 2 TBSP SUNFLOWER OIL
- 450 G/1 LB CARROTS, GRATED
- 225 G/8 OZ LEEKS, SHREDDED
- 2 ORANGES, PEELED AND SEGMENTED
- 2 TBSP TOMATO KETCHUP
- 1 TBSP DEMERARA SUGAR
- 2 TBSP LIGHT SOY SAUCE
- 100 G/3½ OZ CHOPPED PEANUTS

1 Heat the sunflower oil in a large preheated wok.

2 Add the grated carrot and leeks to the wok and stir-fry for 2–3 minutes, or until the vegetables are just soft.

3 Add the orange segments to the wok and heat through gently, ensuring that you do not break up the orange segments as you stir the mixture.

4 Mix the tomato ketchup, sugar and soy sauce together in a small bowl.

5 Add the tomato ketchup mixture to the wok and stir-fry for a further 2 minutes.

6 Transfer the stir-fry to warmed serving bowls and scatter over the chopped peanuts. Serve immediately.

GARLIC MASH

INGREDIENTS

- 900 G/2 LB FLOURY POTATOES, CUT INTO CHUNKS
- 8 GARLIC CLOVES, CRUSHED
- 150 ML/5 FL OZ MILK
- 85 G/3 OZ BUTTER
- PINCH OF FRESHLY GRATED NUTMEG
- SALT AND PEPPER

1 Place the potatoes in a large saucepan with enough water to cover and a pinch of salt. Bring to the boil and cook for 10 minutes. Add the garlic and cook for a further 10–15 minutes, or until the potatoes are tender.

2 Drain the potatoes and garlic, reserving 3 tablespoons of the cooking liquid. Return the reserved cooking liquid to the saucepan, then add the milk and bring to simmering point. Add the butter, return the potatoes and garlic to the saucepan and turn off the heat. Mash thoroughly with a potato masher.

3 Season the potato mixture to taste with nutmeg, salt and pepper and beat thoroughly with a wooden spoon until light and fluffy. Serve immediately.

ROASTED POTATO WEDGES WITH SHALLOTS & ROSEMARY

SERVES 4

INGREDIENTS

- 1 KG/2 LB 4 OZ SMALL OLD POTATOES
- 6 TBSP SPANISH OLIVE OIL
- 2 SPRIGS FRESH ROSEMARY
- 150 G/5½ OZ BABY SHALLOTS
- 2 GARLIC CLOVES, SLICED
- SALT AND PEPPER

1 Preheat the oven to 200°C/400°F/Gas Mark 6. Peel and cut each potato into 8 thick wedges. Put the potatoes in a large saucepan of lightly salted water and bring to the boil. Reduce the heat and simmer for 5 minutes.

2 Heat the oil in a large roasting tin on the hob. Drain the potatoes well and add to the roasting tin. Strip the leaves from the rosemary sprigs, chop finely and sprinkle over the potatoes.

3 Roast the potatoes in the preheated oven for 35 minutes, turning twice during cooking. Add the shallots and garlic and roast for a further 15 minutes until golden brown. Season to taste with salt and pepper.

4 Transfer to a warmed serving dish and serve hot.

CARAMELIZED SWEET POTATOES

SERVES 4

INGREDIENTS

- 450 G/1 LB SWEET POTATOES
- 55 G/2 OZ BUTTER
- 55 G/2 OZ BROWN SUGAR, MAPLE SYRUP OR HONEY
- 2 TBSP ORANGE OR PINEAPPLE JUICE
- 55 G/2 OZ PINEAPPLE PIECES (OPTIONAL)
- PINCH OF GROUND CINNAMON, NUTMEG OR MIXED SPICE (OPTIONAL)

1 Wash the sweet potatoes, but do not peel. Bring a large saucepan of lightly salted water to the boil, add the sweet potatoes and boil until just tender, for about 30–45 minutes, depending on their size. Remove from the heat and drain well. Cool slightly, then peel.

2 Preheat the oven to 200°C/400°F/Gas Mark 6.

3 Thickly slice the sweet potatoes and arrange in a single overlapping layer in a greased ovenproof dish. Cut the butter into small cubes and dot over the top.

4 Sprinkle with the sugar and fruit juice. Add the pineapple and spices, if using.

5 Bake for 30–40 minutes, basting occasionally, until golden brown.

ROASTED ROOT VEGETABLES

SERVES 4–6

INGREDIENTS

- 3 PARSNIPS, CUT INTO
  5-CM/2-INCH CHUNKS
- 4 BABY TURNIPS, CUT INTO
  QUARTERS
- 3 CARROTS, CUT INTO
  5-CM/2-INCH CHUNKS
- 450 G/1 LB BUTTERNUT
  SQUASH, PEELED AND CUT
  INTO 5-CM/2-INCH CHUNKS
- 450 G/1 LB SWEET POTATOES,
  PEELED AND CUT INTO
  5-CM/2-INCH CHUNKS
- 2 GARLIC CLOVES, FINELY
  CHOPPED
- 2 TBSP CHOPPED FRESH
  ROSEMARY
- 2 TBSP CHOPPED FRESH THYME
- 2 TSP CHOPPED FRESH SAGE
- 3 TBSP OLIVE OIL
- SALT AND PEPPER
- 2 TBSP CHOPPED FRESH MIXED
  HERBS, SUCH AS PARSLEY,
  THYME AND MINT,
  TO GARNISH

1. Preheat the oven to 220°C/425°F/ Gas Mark 7.

2. Arrange all the vegetables in a single layer in a large roasting tin. Scatter over the garlic and the herbs. Pour over the oil and season well with salt and pepper.

3. Toss all the ingredients together until they are well mixed and coated with the oil (you can leave them to marinate at this stage to allow the flavours to be absorbed).

4. Roast the vegetables at the top of the oven for 50–60 minutes until they are cooked and nicely browned. Turn the vegetables over halfway through the cooking time. Serve with a good handful of fresh herbs scattered on top and a final sprinkling of salt and pepper to taste.

BAKED CELERY WITH CREAM

SERVES 4

INGREDIENTS

- 1 HEAD OF CELERY
- ½ TSP GROUND CUMIN
- ½ TSP GROUND CORIANDER
- 1 GARLIC CLOVE, CRUSHED
- 1 RED ONION, THINLY SLICED
- 50 G/1¾ OZ PECAN NUTS, HALVED
- 150 ML/5 FL OZ VEGETABLE STOCK
- 150 ML/5 FL OZ SINGLE CREAM
- 50 G/1¾ OZ FRESH WHOLEMEAL BREADCRUMBS
- 25 G/1 OZ FRESHLY GRATED PARMESAN CHEESE
- SALT AND PEPPER

1 Preheat the oven to 200°C/400°F/ Gas Mark 6. Trim the celery and cut into matchsticks. Place the celery in an ovenproof dish with the cumin, coriander, garlic, red onion and pecan nuts.

2 Mix the stock and cream together in a jug and pour over the vegetables. Season to taste with salt and pepper. Mix the breadcrumbs and cheese together in a small bowl and sprinkle over the top to cover the vegetables.

3 Cook in the preheated oven for 40 minutes, or until the vegetables are tender and the top is crispy. Serve immediately.

ASPARAGUS WITH SWEET TOMATO DRESSING

SERVES 4

INGREDIENTS

- 5 TBSP EXTRA VIRGIN OLIVE OIL, PLUS EXTRA FOR BRUSHING
- 55 G/2 OZ PINE KERNELS
- 350 G/12 OZ TOMATOES, PEELED, DESEEDED AND CHOPPED
- 2 TBSP BALSAMIC VINEGAR
- 500 G/1 LB 2 OZ YOUNG ASPARAGUS SPEARS, TRIMMED
- 25 G/1 OZ PARMESAN CHEESE, THINLY SHAVED
- SALT AND PEPPER

1 Brush the grill with oil and preheat. Dry-fry the pine nuts in a heavy-based frying pan for 30–60 seconds, until golden. Tip into a bowl and set aside.

2 Mix together the tomatoes, vinegar and olive oil in a bowl and season with salt and pepper. Set aside.

3 When the grill is hot add the asparagus spears and cook for 3–4 minutes until tender. Carefully transfer to a serving dish. Spoon over the dressing, sprinkle with the pine kernels and Parmesan shavings and serve immediately.

ASPARAGUS & SUN-DRIED TOMATO RISOTTO

SERVES 4

INGREDIENTS

- 1 LITRE/1¾ PINTS VEGETABLE STOCK
- 1 TBSP OLIVE OIL
- 40 G/1½ OZ BUTTER
- 1 SMALL ONION, FINELY CHOPPED
- 6 SUN-DRIED TOMATOES, THINLY SLICED
- 280 G/10 OZ RISOTTO RICE
- 150 ML/5 FL OZ DRY WHITE WINE
- 225 G/8 OZ FRESH ASPARAGUS SPEARS, COOKED
- 85 G/3 OZ FRESHLY GRATED PARMESAN OR GRANA PADANO CHEESE, THINLY PARED, PLUS EXTRA TO GARNISH
- SALT AND PEPPER
- LEMON RIND, TO GARNISH

1 Bring the stock to the boil in a saucepan, then reduce the heat and keep simmering gently over a low heat while you are cooking the risotto.

2 Heat the oil with 25 g/1 oz of the butter in a deep saucepan over a medium heat until the butter has melted.

3 Stir in the onion and sun-dried tomatoes, and cook, stirring occasionally, for 5 minutes, until the onion is soft and starting to turn golden. Do not brown.

4 Reduce the heat, add the rice and mix to coat in oil and butter. Cook, stirring constantly, for 2–3 minutes, or until the grains are translucent.

5 Add the wine and cook, stirring constantly, until it has reduced.

6 Gradually add the hot stock, a ladleful at a time. Stir constantly and add more liquid as the rice absorbs each addition. Increase the heat to medium so that the liquid bubbles. Cook for 20 minutes, or until all the liquid is absorbed and the rice is creamy. Season to taste.

7 While the risotto is cooking, cut most of the asparagus into pieces about 2.5 cm/ 1 inch long. Keep several spears whole for garnishing the finished dish. Carefully fold the cut pieces of asparagus into the risotto for the last 5 minutes of cooking time.

8 Remove the risotto from the heat and add the remaining butter. Mix well, then stir in the Parmesan until it melts. Spoon the risotto on to individual warmed serving dishes and garnish with whole spears of asparagus. Sprinkle some Parmesan and lemon rind on top and serve.

BEANSPROUT SALAD

SERVES 4

INGREDIENTS

- 350 G/12 OZ BEANSPROUTS
- 1 SMALL CUCUMBER
- 1 GREEN PEPPER, DESEEDED AND CUT INTO MATCHSTICKS
- 1 CARROT, CUT INTO MATCHSTICKS
- 2 TOMATOES, FINELY CHOPPED
- 1 CELERY STICK, CUT INTO MATCHSTICKS
- 1 GARLIC CLOVE, CRUSHED
- DASH OF CHILLI SAUCE
- 2 TBSP LIGHT SOY SAUCE
- 1 TSP WINE VINEGAR
- 2 TSP SESAME OIL
- FRESH CHIVES, TO GARNISH

1 Blanch the beansprouts in boiling water for 1 minute. Drain well and rinse under cold water. Drain thoroughly again.

2 Cut the cucumber in half lengthways. Scoop out the seeds with a teaspoon and discard. Cut the flesh into matchsticks and mix with the beansprouts, green pepper, carrot, tomatoes and celery.

3 Mix together the garlic, chilli sauce, soy sauce, vinegar and sesame oil. Pour the dressing over the vegetables, tossing well to coat. Spoon on to 4 individual serving plates. Garnish with fresh chives and serve.

STIR-FRIED BEANSPROUTS

SERVES 4

INGREDIENTS

- 1 TBSP VEGETABLE OR GROUNDNUT OIL
- 225 G/8 OZ BEANSPROUTS, TRIMMED
- 2 TBSP FINELY CHOPPED SPRING ONION
- $1/2$ TSP SALT
- PINCH OF SUGAR

1 In a preheated wok or deep saucepan, heat the oil and stir-fry the beansprouts with the spring onion for about 1 minute. Add the salt and sugar and stir. Remove from the heat and serve immediately.

FENNEL RISOTTO WITH VODKA

SERVES 4–5

INGREDIENTS

- 2 LARGE FENNEL BULBS
- 2 TBSP VEGETABLE OIL
- 6 TBSP UNSALTED BUTTER
- 1 LARGE ONION, FINELY CHOPPED
- 350 G/12 OZ ARBORIO OR CARNAROLI RICE
- 150 ML/5 FL OZ VODKA OR LEMON-FLAVOURED VODKA
- 1.3 LITRES/2^1/4 PINTS VEGETABLE STOCK, SIMMERING (SEE PAGE 36)
- 55 G/2 OZ PARMESAN CHEESE, FRESHLY GRATED
- 5–6 TBSP LEMON JUICE

1 Trim the fennel, reserving the fronds for the garnish, if wished. Cut the bulbs in half lengthways, remove the V-shaped cores and roughly chop the flesh. (If you like, add the fennel trimmings to the stock for extra flavour.)

2 Heat the oil and half the butter in a large heavy-based saucepan over a medium heat. Add the onion and fennel and cook for about 2 minutes, stirring frequently, until the vegetables are soft. Add the rice and cook for about 2 minutes, stirring frequently, or until the rice is translucent and well coated.

3 Pour the vodka into the saucepan: it will bubble rapidly and evaporate almost immediately. Add a ladleful of the vegetable stock. Cook, stirring constantly with a spoon, until all the stock has been absorbed.

4 Continue stirring in the stock, about half a ladleful at a time, allowing each addition to be absorbed by the rice before adding the next. This should take about 20–25 minutes. The finished risotto should have a creamy consistency, and the rice grains should be just tender, but firm to the bite.

5 Stir in the remaining butter, with the grated Parmesan cheese and lemon juice. Remove from the heat, cover and leave to stand for 1 minute before serving. Garnish with a few of the reserved fennel fronds, if wished.

FRUITS &
SQUASHES

Take advantage of the wide selection of tomatoes, peppers and squashes that are now commonplace in markets and in supermarkets with these exciting recipes. Aubergines, butternut squash, courgettes, peppers, pumpkins and tomatoes come in a variety of colours and shapes, but they all stand up well to long, gentle cooking and respond well to spicing, making them ideal for soups, pasta sauces and curries. The smooth, creamy texture of avocados can be transformed into delicious dips and soups.

DIRECTORY OF FRUITS & SQUASHES

Tomatoes, aubergines, chillies, avocados and peppers are all vegetables, but botanically they are classified as fruits, which distinguishes them from roots, shoots and flowering vegetables. This group includes some of the most versatile vegetables, suitable for most cooking methods – many of them can also be eaten raw.

Fruit vegetables
This nutritious group adds plenty of colour and flavour to a range of dishes.

Aubergines
Known in the Middle East as 'poor man's caviar', aubergines give substance and flavour to spicy stews and tomato-based bakes, and can be roasted, grilled or puréed into garlicky dips.

Tomatoes
There are now so many varieties of tomato from which to choose, from the sweet, bite-sized cherry to the large beef. The egg-shaped plum tomato makes rich sauces, while sun-dried tomatoes add a sweet richness to dips, sauces, soups and stews.

Chillies
Chillies have a crucial role in many cuisines, including Mexican, Indian and Thai. There are hundreds of different types, which range in potency from the mild and flavourful to the blisteringly hot.

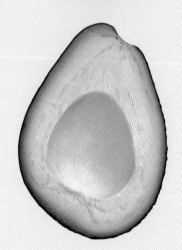

Peppers
Red, yellow and orange peppers are an excellent source of vitamin C, green and purple to a lesser extent. Green peppers are fully developed, but are not as ripe as their more colourful counterparts, which can make them relatively difficult to digest.

Avocados
Avocados are rich in vitamins C and E and are said to improve the condition of the skin and hair. Brush them with lemon or lime juice after cutting to prevent the flesh discolouring. They

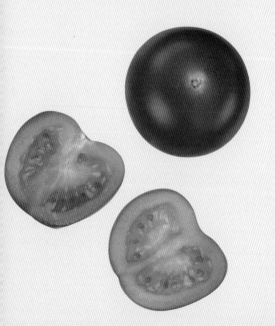

are usually served raw, but can also be baked.

Pumpkin and squash

This group of vegetables comes in a wide range of colours, shapes and sizes. They are broadly divided into two types: summer, which include cucumbers, courgettes and marrows; and winter, such as the various pumpkins and squashes.

Summer

Courgettes are at their best when small and young; the flavour diminishes and the seeds toughen as they grow older and larger. Extremely versatile, courgettes can be steamed, stir-fried, puréed, griddled and roasted, as well as used in soups and casseroles. Their deep yellow flowers are perfect for stuffing. Look for firm, bright, unblemished vegetables that are heavy for their size.

Winter

Butternut squash is one of the most readily available winter types. A large, distinctively pear-shaped vegetable with a golden skin and orange flesh, it is equally delicious mashed, baked or roasted, or used in soups and stews, and makes a good substitute for pumpkin. Small pumpkins have a sweeter, less fibrous flesh than the large ones, which are probably best kept for making lanterns at Halloween!

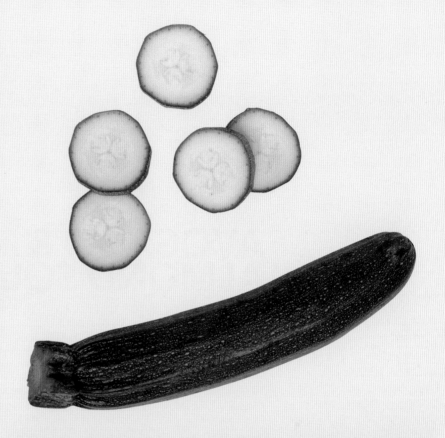

How to Prepare Pumpkin and Squash

These vegetables have thick skins, which are usually removed before cooking. Select a large, heavy knife and put a damp tea towel under the chopping board so that it doesn't slip. Cut off a slice from the bottom, to give you a flat base, and cut off the stalk end, too. Stand the vegetable on the base and cut away the tough skin with firm, vertical slices for butternut squash or following the curve for round varieties and pumpkins. Then slice in half and use a large spoon to scrape out all the seeds and fibres. Dice or slice the flesh.

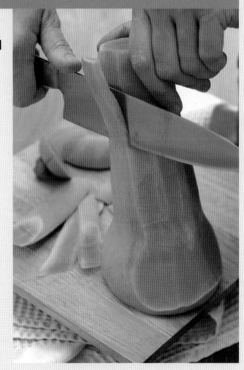

AVOCADO & ALMOND SOUP

SERVES 4

INGREDIENTS

- 600 ML/1 PINT WATER
- 1 ONION, FINELY CHOPPED
- 1 CELERY STICK, FINELY CHOPPED
- 1 CARROT, GRATED
- 4 GARLIC CLOVES, CHOPPED OR CRUSHED
- 1 BAY LEAF
- 100 G/3½ OZ GROUND ALMONDS
- 2 RIPE AVOCADOS (ABOUT 450 G/1 LB TOTAL WEIGHT)
- 3–4 TBSP FRESH LEMON JUICE
- SALT
- SNIPPED FRESH CHIVES, TO GARNISH

1 Combine the water, onion, celery, carrot, garlic, bay leaf and ½ teaspoon salt in a pan. Bring to the boil, reduce the heat, cover and simmer for about 30 minutes or until the vegetables are very tender.

2 Strain the mixture, reserving the liquid and the vegetables separately. Remove and discard the bay leaf.

3 Put the vegetables into a blender or food processor. Add the almonds and a small amount of the liquid and process to a very smooth purée, scraping down the sides as necessary. Add as much of the remaining liquid as the capacity of the blender or processor permits and process to combine. Scrape into a bowl, stir in any remaining liquid, cover and chill until cold.

4 Cut the avocados in half, discard the stones and scoop the flesh into the blender or food processor. Add the cold soup base and process to a smooth purée, scraping down the sides as necessary. For a thinner consistency, add a few spoonfuls of cold water.

5 Add the lemon juice and season with salt to taste. Ladle into chilled small bowls and sprinkle each serving lightly with chives.

GUACAMOLE

SERVES 4

INGREDIENTS

- 1 RIPE TOMATO
- 2 LIMES
- 2–3 RIPE SMALL TO MEDIUM AVOCADOS, OR 1–2 LARGE ONES
- ¼– ½ ONION, FINELY CHOPPED
- PINCH OF GROUND CUMIN
- PINCH OF MILD CHILLI POWDER
- ½–1 FRESH GREEN CHILLI, SUCH AS JALAPEÑO OR SERRANO, DESEEDED AND FINELY CHOPPED
- 1 TBSP FINELY CHOPPED FRESH CORIANDER LEAVES, PLUS EXTRA FOR GARNISHING
- SALT (OPTIONAL)
- TORTILLA CHIPS, TO SERVE (OPTIONAL)

1 Place the tomatoes in a heatproof bowl, pour over boiling water to cover and leave for 30 seconds. Drain and plunge into cold water. Peel off the skins. Cut the tomatoes in half, deseed and chop the flesh.

2 Squeeze the juice from the limes into a small bowl. Cut 1 avocado in half around the stone. Twist the 2 halves apart in opposite directions, then remove the stone with a knife. Carefully peel off the skin, dice the flesh and toss in the bowl of lime juice to prevent the flesh discolouring. Repeat with the remaining avocados. Mash the avocados coarsely with a fork.

3 Add the onion, tomato, cumin, chilli powder, chillies and coriander to the avocados. If using as a dip for tortilla chips, do not add salt. If using as a dip for vegetable sticks, add salt to taste.

4 To serve the guacamole, transfer to a serving dish, garnish with coriander and serve with the tortilla chips, if using.

CUCUMBER & TOMATO SOUP

SERVES 6

INGREDIENTS

- 4 TOMATOES, PEELED AND DESEEDED
- 1.5 KG/3 LB 5 OZ WATERMELON, SEEDLESS IF AVAILABLE
- 10-CM/4-INCH PIECE OF CUCUMBER, PEELED AND DESEEDED
- 2 SPRING ONIONS, GREEN PART ONLY, CHOPPED
- 1 TBSP CHOPPED FRESH MINT
- SALT AND PEPPER
- FRESH MINT SPRIGS, TO GARNISH

1 Remove the rind from the melon, and remove the seeds if it is not seedless.

2 Put the tomatoes into a blender or food processor and, with the motor running, add the cucumber, spring onions, watermelon and mint. Season to taste with salt and pepper and blend until smooth.

3 If you are not using a blender or food processor, push the watermelon through a sieve. Dice the tomatoes and add them to the melon mixture with the mint and salt and pepper to taste. Finely chop the cucumber and spring onions and add to the mixture.

4 Chill the soup overnight the refrigerator. Check the seasoning and transfer to a serving dish. Garnish with the mint sprigs and serve.

TOMATO & ROSEMARY FOCACCIA

MAKES 1 LOAF

INGREDIENTS

- 500 G/1 LB 2 OZ STRONG WHITE BREAD FLOUR, PLUS EXTRA FOR DUSTING
- 1½ TSP SALT
- 1½ TSP EASY-BLEND DRIED YEAST
- 2 TBSP CHOPPED FRESH ROSEMARY, PLUS EXTRA SPRIGS TO GARNISH
- 6 TBSP EXTRA VIRGIN OLIVE OIL, PLUS EXTRA FOR BRUSHING
- 300 ML/10 FL OZ LUKEWARM WATER
- 6 OVEN-DRIED OR SUN-BLUSH TOMATO HALVES
- 1 TSP COARSE SEA SALT

1 Sift the flour and salt together into a bowl and stir in the yeast and rosemary. Make a well in the centre, pour in 4 tbsp of the olive oil and mix quickly with a wooden spoon. Gradually stir in the lukewarm water but do not overmix. Turn out on to a lightly floured surface and knead for 2 minutes. The dough will be quite wet; do not add more flour.

2 Brush a bowl with oil. Shape the dough into a ball, put it into the bowl and put the bowl into a plastic bag or cover with a damp tea towel. Leave to rise in a warm place for 2 hours, until doubled in volume.

3 Brush a baking sheet with oil. Turn out the dough on to a lightly floured surface and knock back with your fist, then knead for 1 minute. Put the dough on to the prepared baking sheet and press out into an even layer. Put the baking sheet into a plastic bag or cover with a damp tea towel. Leave to rise in a warm place for 1 hour.

4 Preheat the oven to 240°C/475°F/ Gas Mark 9. Cut the tomato halves in half. Whisk the remaining oil with a little water in a bowl. Dip your fingers into the oil mixture and press them into the dough to make dimples all over the loaf. Sprinkle with the sea salt. Press the tomato quarters into some of the dimples, drizzle with the remaining oil mixture and sprinkle the loaf with the rosemary sprigs.

5 Lower the oven temperature to 220°C/ 425°F/Gas Mark 7 and bake the focaccia for 20 minutes, until golden brown. Transfer to a wire rack to cool slightly, then serve while still warm. Alternatively, allow the loaf to cool completely and reheat in a low oven before serving.

PEPPERS WITH FETA

MAKES 12

INGREDIENTS

- 125 G/4½ OZ FETA CHEESE (DRAINED WEIGHT)
- 12 LONG, SLENDER RED OR YELLOW PEPPERS OR SHORT, THICK FRESH RED CHILLIES, RUBBED WITH OLIVE OIL
- EXTRA VIRGIN OLIVE OIL, FOR DRIZZLING
- PEPPER

1 Put the cheese in a bowl with warm water to cover. Leave to soak for 1 hour, changing the water 2–3 times.

2 Meanwhile, preheat the grill to its highest setting. Put the peppers in a roasting tin and cook under the grill, about 10 cm/ 4 inches from the heat, for 10 minutes, turning once, until the skins are just charred. Transfer to a bowl, cover with a folded clean tea towel and leave to cool.

3 When cool enough to handle, peel away the skins, then cut off the tips so that they are about 4 cm/1½ inches long. Use a teaspoon to scrape out the seeds and membranes from the pepper tips, being careful not to tear the flesh.

4 Put the drained cheese in a bowl and use a fork to mash into a thick paste. Put 1 teaspoon of the cheese in each pepper tip and use your fingers to push it into the cavity, handling gently to prevent tearing. Put on a serving plate, drizzle with oil and season to taste with pepper. Cover and chill in the refrigerator until ready to serve.

TOMATO & POTATO TORTILLA

SERVES 6

INGREDIENTS

- 1 KG/2 LB 4 OZ POTATOES, PEELED AND CUT INTO SMALL CUBES
- 2 TBSP OLIVE OIL
- 1 BUNCH SPRING ONIONS, CHOPPED
- 115 G/4 OZ CHERRY TOMATOES
- 6 EGGS
- 3 TBSP WATER
- 2 TBSP CHOPPED FRESH PARSLEY
- SALT AND PEPPER

1 Cook the potatoes in a saucepan of lightly salted boiling water for 8–10 minutes, or until tender. Drain and reserve until required.

2 Preheat the grill to medium. Heat the oil in a large frying pan. Add the spring onions and fry until just soft. Add the potatoes and fry for 3–4 minutes, until coated with oil and hot. Smooth the top and scatter over the tomatoes.

3 Mix the eggs, water, salt and pepper and parsley together in a bowl, then pour into the frying pan. Cook over a very gentle heat for 10–15 minutes, until the tortilla looks fairly set.

4 Place the frying pan under the hot grill and cook until the top is brown and set. Leave to cool for 10–15 minutes before sliding out of the frying pan on to a chopping board. Cut into wedges and serve immediately.

PASTA SALAD WITH CHARGRILLED PEPPERS

SERVES 4

INGREDIENTS

- 1 RED PEPPER
- 1 ORANGE PEPPER
- 280 G/10 OZ DRIED CONCHIGLIE
- 5 TBSP EXTRA VIRGIN OLIVE OIL
- 2 TBSP LEMON JUICE
- 2 TBSP PESTO SAUCE
  (SEE PAGE 37)
- 1 GARLIC CLOVE, FINELY
  CHOPPED
- 3 TBSP SHREDDED FRESH BASIL
  LEAVES
- SALT AND PEPPER

1 Preheat the grill. Put the whole peppers on a baking sheet and place under the hot grill, turning frequently, for 15 minutes, or until charred all over. Remove with tongs and place in a bowl. Cover with crumpled kitchen paper and reserve.

2 Meanwhile, bring a large saucepan of lightly salted water to the boil. Add the pasta, return to the boil and cook for 8–10 minutes, or until the pasta is tender but still firm to the bite.

3 Combine the olive oil, lemon juice, Pesto Sauce and garlic in a bowl, whisking well to mix. Drain the pasta, add it to the pesto mixture while still hot and toss well. Reserve until required.

4 When the peppers are cool enough to handle, peel off the skins, then cut open and remove the seeds. Chop the flesh roughly and add to the pasta with the basil. Season to taste with salt and pepper and toss well. Serve.

COURGETTE & BASIL RISOTTO

SERVES 4

INGREDIENTS

- 4 TBSP BASIL-FLAVOURED EXTRA VIRGIN OLIVE OIL, PLUS EXTRA FOR DRIZZLING
- 4 COURGETTES, DICED
- 1 YELLOW PEPPER, DESEEDED AND DICED
- 2 GARLIC CLOVES, FINELY CHOPPED
- 1 LARGE ONION, FINELY CHOPPED
- 400 G/14 OZ ARBORIO OR CARNAROLI RICE
- 4 TBSP DRY WHITE VERMOUTH
- 1.5 LITRES/2¾ PINTS VEGETABLE STOCK, SIMMERING (SEE PAGE 36)
- 2 TBSP UNSALTED BUTTER, AT ROOM TEMPERATURE
- LARGE HANDFUL OF FRESH BASIL LEAVES, TORN, PLUS A FEW LEAVES TO GARNISH
- 85 G/3 OZ PARMESAN CHEESE, FRESHLY GRATED

1 Heat half the olive oil in a large frying pan over a high heat. When very hot, but not smoking, add the diced courgettes and yellow pepper and stir-fry for 3 minutes until lightly golden. Stir in the chopped garlic and cook for a further 30 seconds. Transfer to a plate and set aside.

2 Heat the remaining oil in a large heavy-based saucepan over a medium heat. Add the onion and cook, stirring occasionally, for about 2 minutes, until soft. Add the rice and cook, stirring frequently, for about 2 minutes, until the rice is translucent and well coated with the oil.

3 Pour in the vermouth; it will bubble and steam rapidly and evaporate almost immediately. Add a ladleful of the simmering stock and cook, stirring constantly until the stock has been completely absorbed.

4 Continue adding the stock, about half a ladleful at a time, allowing each addition to be absorbed before adding the next. This should take 20–25 minutes. The risotto should have a creamy consistency and the rice should be tender, but still firm to the bite.

5 Stir in the courgette mixture with any juices, the butter, basil and grated Parmesan cheese. Drizzle with a little oil and garnish with basil. Serve hot.

PASTA ALL'ARRABBIATA

SERVES 4

INGREDIENTS

- 150 ML/5 FL OZ DRY WHITE WINE
- 1 TBSP SUN-DRIED TOMATO PURÉE
- 2 FRESH RED CHILLIES
- 2 GARLIC CLOVES, FINELY CHOPPED
- 350 G/12 OZ DRIED TORTIGLIONI
- 4 TBSP CHOPPED FRESH FLAT-LEAF PARSLEY
- SALT AND PEPPER
- FRESH PECORINO CHEESE SHAVINGS, TO GARNISH

SUGOCASA
- 5 TBSP EXTRA VIRGIN OLIVE OIL
- 450 G/1 LB PLUM TOMATOES, CHOPPED
- SALT AND PEPPER

1 Make the Sugocasa. Heat the oil in a frying pan over a high heat until almost smoking. Add the tomatoes and cook, stirring frequently, for 2–3 minutes. Reduce the heat to low and cook gently for 20 minutes, or until very soft. Season to taste with salt and pepper. Using a wooden spoon, press through a non-metallic sieve into a saucepan.

2 Add the wine, tomato purée, whole chillies and garlic to the Sugocasa and bring to the boil. Reduce the heat and simmer gently.

3 Meanwhile, bring a large saucepan of lightly salted water to the boil. Add the pasta, return to the boil and cook for 8–10 minutes, until the pasta is tender but still firm to the bite.

4 Remove the chillies and taste the sauce. If you prefer a hotter flavour, chop some or all of the chillies and return to the saucepan. Check and adjust the seasoning, if necessary, then stir in half the parsley.

5 Drain the pasta and transfer to a warmed serving bowl. Add the sauce and toss to coat. Sprinkle with the remaining parsley, garnish with the cheese shavings and serve at once.

CHILLI TOFU TORTILLAS

MAKES 8

INGREDIENTS

- ½ TSP CHILLI POWDER
- 1 TSP PAPRIKA
- 2 TBSP PLAIN FLOUR
- SALT AND PEPPER
- 225 G/8 OZ FIRM TOFU, CUT INTO 1-CM/½-INCH PIECES
- 2 TBSP VEGETABLE OIL
- 1 ONION, FINELY CHOPPED
- 1 GARLIC CLOVE, CRUSHED
- 1 LARGE RED PEPPER, DESEEDED AND FINELY CHOPPED
- 1 LARGE RIPE AVOCADO
- 1 TBSP LIME JUICE
- 4 TOMATOES, PEELED, DESEEDED AND CHOPPED
- 125 G/4½ OZ CHEDDAR CHEESE, GRATED
- 8 SOFT FLOUR TORTILLAS
- 150 ML/5 FL OZ SOURED CREAM
- PICKLED GREEN JALAPEÑO CHILLIES, TO SERVE

SAUCE

- 850 ML/1½ PINTS SUGOCASA (SEE PAGE 97)
- 3 TBSP CHOPPED FRESH PARSLEY
- 3 TBSP CHOPPED FRESH CORIANDER

1 Preheat the oven to 190°C/375°F/Gas Mark 5. Mix the chilli powder, paprika, flour, and salt and pepper to taste, on a plate and coat the tofu pieces.

2 Heat the oil in a frying pan and gently fry the tofu for 3–4 minutes, until golden. Remove with a slotted spoon, drain on kitchen paper and set aside.

3 Add the onion, garlic and pepper to the oil and fry for 2–3 minutes, until just soft. Drain and set aside.

4 Halve the avocado, peel, and remove the stone. Slice lengthways, put in a bowl with the lime juice and toss to coat.

5 Add the tofu and the onion mixture and gently stir in the chopped tomatoes and half the cheese. Spoon one-eighth of the filling down the centre of each tortilla, top with soured cream and roll up.

6 Arrange the tortillas in a shallow ovenproof dish in a single layer.

7 To make the sauce, mix all the ingredients together. Spoon the sauce over the tortillas, sprinkle with the remaining grated cheese and bake in the preheated oven for 25 minutes, until the cheese is golden brown and bubbling.

8 Serve the tortillas immediately with the pickled jalapeño chillies.

RADIATORI WITH PUMPKIN SAUCE

SERVES 4

INGREDIENTS

- 55 G/2 OZ UNSALTED BUTTER
- 115 G/4 OZ WHITE ONIONS OR SHALLOTS, VERY FINELY CHOPPED
- 800 G/1 LB 12 OZ PUMPKIN, UNPREPARED WEIGHT
- PINCH OF FRESHLY GRATED NUTMEG
- 350 G/12 OZ DRIED RADIATORI
- 200 ML/7 FL OZ SINGLE CREAM
- 4 TBSP FRESHLY GRATED PARMESAN CHEESE, PLUS EXTRA TO SERVE
- 2 TBSP CHOPPED FRESH FLAT-LEAF PARSLEY
- SALT AND PEPPER

1 Melt the butter in a heavy-based saucepan over a low heat. Add the onions, sprinkle with a little salt, cover and cook, stirring frequently, for 25–30 minutes.

2 Scoop out and discard the pumpkin seeds. Peel and finely chop the flesh. Tip the pumpkin into the saucepan and season to taste with nutmeg. Cover and cook over a low heat, stirring occasionally, for 45 minutes.

3 Meanwhile, bring a large saucepan of lightly salted water to the boil. Add the pasta, return to the boil and cook for 8–10 minutes, or until the pasta is tender but still firm to the bite. Drain thoroughly, reserving about 150 ml/5 fl oz of the cooking liquid.

4 Stir the cream, cheese and parsley into the pumpkin sauce and season to taste with salt and pepper. If the mixture seems a little too thick, add some or all of the reserved cooking liquid and stir. Tip in the pasta and toss for 1 minute. Serve immediately, with Parmesan cheese for sprinkling.

PUMPKIN CHESTNUT RISOTTO

SERVES 4

INGREDIENTS

- 1 LITRE/1¾ PINTS VEGETABLE STOCK (SEE PAGE 36)
- 1 TBSP OLIVE OIL
- 40 G/1½ OZ BUTTER
- 1 SMALL ONION, FINELY CHOPPED
- 225 G/8 OZ PUMPKIN, DICED
- 225 G/8 OZ CHESTNUTS, COOKED AND SHELLED
- 280 G/10 OZ RISOTTO RICE
- 150 ML/5 FL OZ DRY WHITE WINE
- 1 TSP CRUMBLED SAFFRON THREADS (OPTIONAL)
- 85 G/3 OZ PARMESAN OR GRANA PADANO CHEESE, FRESHLY GRATED, PLUS EXTRA FOR SERVING
- SALT AND PEPPER

1 Bring the stock to the boil, then reduce the heat and keep simmering gently over a low heat while you are cooking the risotto.

2 Heat the oil with 25 g/1 oz of the butter in a deep saucepan over a medium heat until the butter has melted. Stir in the onion and pumpkin and cook, stirring occasionally, for 5 minutes, or until the onion is soft and starting to turn golden and the pumpkin begins to colour. Roughly chop the chestnuts and add to the mixture. Stir thoroughly to coat.

3 Reduce the heat, add the rice and mix to coat in oil and butter. Cook, stirring constantly, for 2–3 minutes, or until the grains are translucent. Add the wine and cook, stirring constantly, for 1 minute until it has reduced. If using the saffron threads, dissolve them in 4 tablespoons of the hot stock and add the liquid to the rice after the wine has been absorbed. Cook, stirring constantly, until the liquid has been absorbed.

4 Gradually add the hot stock, a ladleful at a time, stirring constantly. Add more liquid as the rice absorbs each addition. Increase the heat to medium so that the liquid bubbles. Cook for 20 minutes, or until all the liquid has been absorbed and the rice is creamy. Season to taste.

5 Remove the risotto from the heat and add the remaining butter. Mix well, then stir in the cheese until it melts. Adjust the seasoning, if necessary, spoon the risotto on to 4 warmed plates and serve immediately, sprinkled with grated cheese.

BUTTERNUT SQUASH
STIR-FRY

SERVES 4

INGREDIENTS

- 1 KG/2 LB 4 OZ BUTTERNUT SQUASH, PEELED
- 3 TBSP GROUNDNUT OIL
- 1 ONION, SLICED
- 2 CLOVES GARLIC, CRUSHED
- 1 TSP CORIANDER SEEDS
- 1 TSP CUMIN SEEDS
- 2 TBSP CHOPPED FRESH CORIANDER
- 150 ML/5 FL OZ COCONUT MILK
- 100 ML/3½ FL OZ WATER
- 100 G/3½ OZ SALTED CASHEW NUTS

TO GARNISH

- FRESHLY GRATED LIME RIND
- FRESH CORIANDER
- LIME SLICES

1 Slice the squash into small, bite-sized cubes, using a sharp knife.

2 Heat the groundnut oil in a large, preheated wok.

3 Add the butternut squash, the onion and the garlic to the wok and stir-fry for 5 minutes.

4 Stir in the coriander seeds, cumin seeds and fresh chopped coriander, and stir-fry for 1 minute.

5 Add the coconut milk and water to the wok and bring to the boil. Cover the wok and leave to simmer for 10–15 minutes, or until the squash is tender.

6 Add the cashew nuts and stir to combine thoroughly.

7 Transfer to warmed serving dishes and garnish with the lime rind, the coriander and the lime slices. Serve immediately.

STUFFED AUBERGINES

SERVES 4

INGREDIENTS

- 225 G/8 OZ DRIED PENNE OR OTHER SHORT PASTA SHAPES
- 4 TBSP OLIVE OIL, PLUS EXTRA FOR BRUSHING
- 2 AUBERGINES
- 1 LARGE ONION, CHOPPED
- 2 GARLIC CLOVES, CRUSHED
- 400 G/14 OZ CANNED CHOPPED TOMATOES
- 2 TSP DRIED OREGANO
- 55 G/2 OZ MOZZARELLA CHEESE, THINLY SLICED
- 25 G/1 OZ PARMESAN CHEESE, FRESHLY GRATED
- 5 TBSP DRY BREADCRUMBS
- SALT AND PEPPER

1 Preheat the oven to 200°C/400°C/Gas Mark 6. Bring a large saucepan of lightly salted water to the boil. Add the pasta and 1 tablespoon of the olive oil, bring back to the boil and cook for 8–10 minutes, or until the pasta is just tender, but still firm to the bite. Drain, return to the pan, cover and keep warm.

2 Cut the aubergines in half lengthways and score around the inside with a sharp knife, being careful not to pierce the shells. Scoop out the flesh with a spoon. Brush the insides of the shells with olive oil. Chop the flesh and set aside.

3 Heat the remaining oil in a frying pan. Fry the onion over a low heat for 5 minutes, until soft. Add the garlic and fry for 1 minute. Add the chopped aubergine and fry, stirring frequently, for 5 minutes. Add the tomatoes and oregano and season to taste with salt and pepper. Bring to the boil and simmer for 10 minutes until thickened. Remove the pan from the heat and stir in the pasta.

4 Brush a baking tray with oil and arrange the aubergine shells in a single layer. Divide half of the tomato and pasta mixture between them. Scatter over the slices of mozzarella cheese, then pile the remaining tomato and pasta mixture on top. Mix the Parmesan cheese and breadcrumbs and sprinkle over the top, patting lightly into the mixture.

5 Bake in the preheated oven for about 25 minutes, or until the topping is golden brown. Serve hot.

AUBERGINE CURRY

SERVES 2

INGREDIENTS

- GROUNDNUT OR VEGETABLE OIL, FOR DEEP-FRYING, PLUS 2 TBSP
- 2 AUBERGINES, CUT INTO 2-CM/¾-INCH CUBES
- 1 BUNCH SPRING ONIONS, ROUGHLY CHOPPED
- 2 GARLIC CLOVES, CHOPPED
- 2 RED PEPPERS, DESEEDED AND CUT INTO 2-CM/¾-INCH SQUARES
- 3 COURGETTES, THICKLY SLICED
- 400 ML/14 FL OZ CANNED COCONUT MILK
- 2 TBSP RED CURRY PASTE
- LARGE HANDFUL OF FRESH CORIANDER, CHOPPED, PLUS EXTRA SPRIGS TO GARNISH
- COOKED RICE OR NOODLES, TO SERVE

1 Heat the oil for deep-frying in a preheated wok or a deep saucepan to 180°C/350°F, or until a cube of bread browns in 30 seconds. Add the aubergine cubes, in batches, and cook for 45 seconds–1 minute until crisp and brown all over. Remove with a slotted spoon and drain on kitchen paper.

2 Heat the remaining 2 tablespoons of oil in a separate preheated wok or large frying pan, add the spring onions and garlic and stir-fry over a medium–high heat for 1 minute. Add the peppers and courgettes and stir-fry for 2–3 minutes. Add the coconut milk and curry paste and bring gently to the boil, stirring occasionally. Add the aubergines and coriander, reduce the heat and simmer for 2–3 minutes.

3 Serve immediately with the rice or noodles, garnished with the coriander sprigs.

POLENTA WITH TOMATOES & GARLIC SAUCE

SERVES 4

INGREDIENTS

- 700 ML/1¼ PINTS VEGETABLE STOCK (SEE PAGE 36) OR WATER
- 175 G/6 OZ QUICK-COOK POLENTA
- 25 G/1 OZ BUTTER
- 3 TBSP SNIPPED FRESH CHIVES
- 2 TBSP CHOPPED FRESH FLAT-LEAF PARSLEY
- OLIVE OIL, FOR BRUSHING
- 4 PLUM TOMATOES, SLICED
- SALT AND PEPPER

GARLIC SAUCE

- 2 THICK SLICES OF FRENCH BREAD, CRUSTS REMOVED
- 3 GARLIC CLOVES, CHOPPED
- ½ TSP SALT
- 115 G/4 OZ WALNUT PIECES
- 3 TBSP LEMON JUICE
- 7 TBSP OLIVE OIL

1 Bring the stock to the boil in a large saucepan and add 1 teaspoon salt. Add the polenta and cook over a medium heat, stirring constantly, for 5 minutes, until it starts to come away from the sides of the pan.

2 Remove the pan from the heat and beat in the butter, chives and parsley and season with pepper. Pour the polenta into a greased dish and spread out evenly. Leave to cool and set.

3 To make the Garlic Sauce, tear the bread into pieces and place in a bowl. Cover with cold water and soak for 10 minutes. Pound the garlic cloves with ½ teaspoon salt to make a paste. Work in the walnuts. Squeeze out the bread, work it into the paste, then work in the lemon juice. Stir in the olive oil until the sauce is thick and creamy. Transfer to a bowl, cover with clingfilm and set aside.

4 Brush the grill with oil and preheat. Cut the set polenta into wedges or rounds. Season the tomatoes with salt and pepper. When the grill is hot add the polenta and tomatoes, and cook for 4–5 minutes.

5 Divide the polenta and tomatoes between warmed plates and spoon over the Garlic Sauce. Serve immediately.

MUSHROOMS & THE ONION FAMILY

If you've fallen into the habit of just sautéeing chopped onion to flavour other ingredients, the recipes in this chapter should make you reconsider your attitude. Like other roots, members of the onion family respond to many culinary treatments and make excellent soups, pasta sauces and Indian-style dishes. Once rare, wild mushrooms are now readily available so use the recipes in this chapter to try a new variety – most are interchangeable so you can always try an alternative type.

DIRECTORY OF MUSHROOMS & ONIONS

The onion has traditionally been used to provide a base for many recipes, although, as this chapter shows, it really comes into its own when served as a vegetable in its own right. The extremely versatile mushroom can be eaten raw in salads, cooked as a vegetable accompaniment or used to flavour a variety of dishes ranging from soups to risottos.

Mushrooms

There is a wide range of mushrooms from which to choose, both fresh and dried, and many types of wild mushroom are now cultivated. The most popular are the mild-flavoured button mushroom and the field mushroom, which has a more earthy, intense flavour. Buy mushrooms that are firm and smell fresh; avoid ones that have slimy, damp patches. Dried mushrooms keep well: to reconstitute them, soak in boiling water for 20–30 minutes. Drain and rinse well to remove any dirt and grit. Use the soaking water in stocks and sauces, but strain first.

Ceps

Ceps have a meaty texture and woody flavour. Dried ceps lend a rich flavour to soups, stocks and sauces.

Chanterelle

Golden-coloured chanterelle (or girolle) mushrooms have a delicate flavour. They should be wiped rather than washed, as they are very porous. Most types of mushroom should be prepared in this way, apart from the honeycomb-capped morel.

Shiitake and oyster

Both shiitake and oyster mushrooms are now widely cultivated. Oyster are fluted in shape, and while they are usually greyish-brown in colour, they also come in pale yellow and pink. Shiitake have a chewy texture and robust flavour, and are most commonly used in Asian dishes.

Onion family

Onions, garlic, leeks, shallots and spring onions add plenty of flavour to all manner of savoury vegetarian dishes and can also be cooked on their own. Onions and garlic should be stored in a cool, dry, airy place away from direct sunlight.

Onions

These provide potent antioxidants and are said to reduce health-threatening cholesterol levels in the body. Cooking tempers the pungency of the onion family, while roasting brings out their delicious sweetness. Onions offer a range of taste sensations from the sweet and mild Spanish white onion and light and fresh spring onion to the versatile and pungent yellow onion. Baby onions and shallots are the smallest.

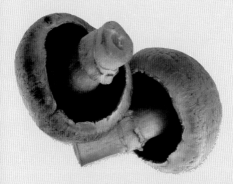

CREAMY MUSHROOM & TARRAGON SOUP

SERVES 4–6

INGREDIENTS

- 50 G/1¾ OZ BUTTER
- 1 ONION, CHOPPED
- 700 G/1 LB 9 OZ BUTTON MUSHROOMS, ROUGHLY CHOPPED
- 850 ML/1½ PINTS VEGETABLE STOCK (SEE PAGE 36)
- 3 TBSP CHOPPED FRESH TARRAGON, PLUS EXTRA TO GARNISH
- 150 ML/5 FL OZ CRÈME FRAÎCHE
- OLIVE OIL, FOR DRIZZLING
- SALT AND PEPPER

1 Melt half the butter in a large saucepan. Add the onion and fry gently for 10 minutes, until soft. Add the remaining butter and the mushrooms and stir-fry for 5 minutes, or until the mushrooms are brown.

2 Stir in the stock and tarragon, bring to the boil, then reduce the heat and leave to simmer gently for 20 minutes. Transfer to a food processor or blender and process until smooth. Return the soup to the pan.

3 Stir in the crème fraîche and add salt and pepper to taste. Reheat the soup gently until hot. Ladle into warmed serving bowls, garnish with tarragon, drizzle with a little olive oil and serve immediately.

WILD MUSHROOM BRUSCHETTA

SERVES 4

INGREDIENTS

- 4 SLICES SOURDOUGH BREAD, SUCH AS PUGLIESE
- 3 GARLIC CLOVES, 1 HALVED AND 2 CRUSHED
- 2 TBSP EXTRA VIRGIAN OLIVE OIL
- 225 G/8 OZ MIXED WILD MUSHROOMS, SUCH AS CEPS, CHANTERELLES AND FIELD MUSHROOMS
- 1 TBSP OLIVE OIL
- 25 G/1 OZ BUTTER
- 1 SMALL ONION OR 2 SHALLOTS, FINELY CHOPPED
- 50 ML/2 FL OZ DRY WHITE WINE OR MARSALA
- SALT AND PEPPER
- 2 TBSP ROUGHLY CHOPPED FRESH FLAT-LEAF PARSLEY, TO GARNISH

1 Preheat the oven to low. Toast the bread slices on both sides under a preheated grill or in a preheated ridged griddle pan, rub with the garlic halves and drizzle with the extra virgin olive oil. Transfer to a baking sheet and keep warm in the preheated oven.

2 Wipe the mushrooms thoroughly to remove any trace of soil and slice any large ones. Heat the olive oil with half the butter in a frying pan, add the mushrooms and cook over a medium heat, stirring frequently, for 3–4 minutes until soft. Remove with a slotted spoon and keep warm in the oven.

3 Heat the remaining butter in the frying pan, add the onion and crushed garlic and cook over a medium heat, stirring frequently, for 3–4 minutes until soft. Add the wine, stir well and leave to bubble for 2–3 minutes until reduced and thickened. Return the mushrooms to the frying pan and heat through. The sauce should be thick enough to glaze the mushrooms. Season to taste with salt and pepper.

4 Pile the mushrooms on top of the warm bruschetta, scatter with the parsley and serve immediately.

MUSHROOM PASTA WITH PORT

SERVES 4

INGREDIENTS

- 55 G/2 OZ BUTTER
- 2 TBSP OLIVE OIL
- 6 SHALLOTS, SLICED
- 450 G/1 LB BUTTON
  MUSHROOMS, SLICED
- 1 TSP PLAIN FLOUR
- 150 ML/5 FL OZ DOUBLE CREAM
- 2 TBSP PORT
- 115 G/4 OZ SUN-DRIED
  TOMATOES, CHOPPED
- FRESHLY GRATED NUTMEG
- 450 G /1 LB DRIED SPAGHETTI
- SALT AND PEPPER
- 1 TBSP CHOPPED FRESH
  PARSLEY, TO GARNISH
- 6 TRIANGLES OF FRIED WHITE
  BREAD, TO SERVE

1 Heat the butter and 1 tablespoon of the oil in a large saucepan. Add the shallots and cook over a medium heat for 3 minutes. Add the mushrooms and cook over a low heat for a further 2 minutes. Season to taste with salt and pepper, sprinkle over the flour and cook, stirring constantly, for 1 minute.

2 Gradually stir in the cream and port, add the sun-dried tomatoes and a pinch of grated nutmeg and cook over a low heat for 8 minutes.

3 Meanwhile, bring a large saucepan of lightly salted water to the boil. Add the spaghetti and remaining olive oil and cook for 12–14 minutes, or until the pasta is tender, but still firm to the bite.

4 Drain the spaghetti and return to the pan. Pour over the mushroom sauce and cook for 3 minutes. Transfer the spaghetti and mushroom sauce to a large serving plate and sprinkle over the chopped parsley. Serve with the triangles of fried bread.

PARMESAN CHEESE RISOTTO WITH MUSHROOMS

SERVES 4

INGREDIENTS

- 1 LITRE/1¾ PINTS VEGETABLE STOCK (SEE PAGE 36)
- 2 TBSP OLIVE OIL OR VEGETABLE OIL
- 225 G/8 OZ RISOTTO RICE
- 2 GARLIC CLOVES, CRUSHED
- 1 ONION, CHOPPED
- 2 CELERY STICKS, CHOPPED
- 1 RED OR GREEN PEPPER, DESEEDED AND CHOPPED
- 225 G/8 OZ MUSHROOMS, THINLY SLICED
- 1 TBSP CHOPPED FRESH OREGANO OR 1 TSP DRIED OREGANO
- 55 G /2 OZ SUN-DRIED TOMATOES IN OLIVE OIL, DRAINED AND CHOPPED (OPTIONAL)
- 55 G/2 OZ FINELY GRATED PARMESAN CHEESE
- SALT AND PEPPER
- CHOPPED FRESH FLAT-LEAF PARSLEY, TO GARNISH

1 Bring the stock to the boil in a saucepan, then reduce the heat and keep simmering gently over a low heat while you are cooking the risotto.

2 Heat the oil in a deep saucepan. Add the rice and cook over a low heat, stirring constantly, for 2–3 minutes, until the grains are thoroughly coated in oil and translucent.

3 Add the garlic, onion, celery and pepper and cook, stirring frequently, for 5 minutes. Add the mushrooms and cook for 3–4 minutes. Stir in the oregano.

4 Gradually add the hot stock, a ladleful at a time. Stir constantly and add more liquid as the rice absorbs each addition. Increase the heat to medium so that the liquid bubbles. Cook for 20 minutes, or until all the liquid is absorbed and the rice is creamy. Add the sun-dried tomatoes, if using, 5 minutes before the end of the cooking time and season to taste with salt and pepper.

5 Remove the risotto from the heat and stir in half the cheese until it melts. Transfer the risotto to warmed plates. Top with the remaining cheese, garnish with the parsley and serve immediately.

MIXED MUSHROOM PIZZA

**MAKES 2 X 23-CM/
9-INCH PIZZAS**

INGREDIENTS

- 3 TBSP OIL
- 2 GARLIC CLOVES, CRUSHED
- 2 TBSP CHOPPED FRESH
  OREGANO
- 2 X 23-CM/9-INCH READY-MADE
  THIN AND CRISPY PIZZA BASES
- 85 G/3 OZ RICOTTA CHEESE
- 1 TBSP MILK
- 40 G/1½ OZ BUTTER
- 350 G/12 OZ MIXED
  MUSHROOMS, SLICED
- 2 TSP LEMON JUICE
- 1 TBSP CHOPPED FRESH
  MARJORAM
- 4 TBSP FRESHLY GRATED
  PARMESAN CHEESE
- SALT AND PEPPER

1 Preheat the oven to 240°C/475°F/Gas Mark 9. Mix 2 tablespoons of the oil, the garlic and oregano together and brush over the pizza bases.

2 Mix the ricotta cheese and milk together in a bowl. Season to taste with salt and pepper and spread the mixture over the pizza bases, leaving a 4-cm/1½-inch border.

3 Heat the butter and the remaining oil together in a large frying pan. Add the mushrooms and cook over a high heat for 2 minutes. Remove the frying pan from the heat, season to taste with salt and pepper and stir in the lemon juice and marjoram.

4 Spoon the mushroom mixture over the pizza bases, leaving a 1-cm/½-inch border. Sprinkle with the grated Parmesan cheese, then bake in the oven for 12–15 minutes, until the crusts are crisp and the mushrooms are cooked. Serve immediately.

RED ONION, TOMATO & HERB SALAD

SERVES 4

INGREDIENTS

- 900 G/2 LB TOMATOES, SLICED THINLY
- 1 TBSP SUGAR, OPTIONAL
- 1 RED ONION, SLICED THINLY
- LARGE HANDFUL OF COARSELY CHOPPED FRESH FLAT-LEAF PARSLEY, TO GARNISH
- SALT AND PEPPER

DRESSING
- 2–4 TBSP VEGETABLE OIL
- 2 TBSP RED WINE VINEGAR OR FRUIT VINEGAR

1 Arrange the tomato slices in a shallow bowl. Sprinkle with sugar (if using), salt and pepper.

2 Separate the onion slices into rings and scatter over the tomatoes. Sprinkle the herbs over the top. Anything that is in season can be used – for example, tarragon, sorrel, coriander or basil.

3 Place the dressing ingredients in a jar with a screw-top lid. Shake well. Pour the dressing over the salad and mix gently.

5 Cover with clingfilm and refrigerate for 20 minutes. Remove the salad from the refrigerator 5 minutes before serving, unwrap the dish and stir gently before setting out on the table.

FLATBREAD WITH ONION & ROSEMARY

MAKES 1 LOAF

INGREDIENTS

- 450 G/1 LB STRONG WHITE FLOUR, PLUS EXTRA FOR DUSTING
- 1½ TSP EASY-BLEND DRIED YEAST
- ½ TSP SALT
- 2 TBSP CHOPPED FRESH ROSEMARY, PLUS EXTRA SMALL SPRIGS TO GARNISH
- 5 TBSP EXTRA VIRGIN OLIVE OIL, PLUS EXTRA FOR OILING
- 300 ML/10 FL OZ WARM WATER
- 1 RED ONION, FINELY SLICED AND SEPARATED INTO RINGS
- 1 TBSP COARSE SEA SALT

1 Mix the flour, yeast and salt together in a mixing bowl, then stir in the chopped rosemary. Make a well in the centre. Mix 3 tablespoons of the oil and water together in a jug and pour into the well. Gradually mix the liquid into the flour mixture with a round-bladed knife. Gather the mixture together with your hands to form a soft dough.

2 Turn out the dough on to a lightly floured work surface and knead for 8–10 minutes until very smooth and elastic. Return the dough to the bowl, cover with a clean tea towel or oiled clingfilm and leave to rise in a warm place for 45 minutes –1 hour, or until doubled in size. Turn out and gently knead again for 1 minute until smooth.

3 Preheat the oven to 200°C/400°F/ Gas Mark 6. Oil a baking sheet. Gently roll out the dough to a round about 30 cm/12 inches in diameter – it doesn't have to be a perfect circle; a slightly oval shape is traditional. Transfer to the prepared baking sheet, cover with a clean tea towel or oiled clingfilm and leave to rise in a warm place for 20–30 minutes.

4 Make holes about 5 cm/2 inches apart all over the surface of the dough with the handle of a wooden spoon. Spread the onion rings over the dough, drizzle with the remaining oil and scatter over the salt. Bake in the preheated oven for 20–25 minutes until well risen and golden brown. Five minutes before the end of the cooking time, garnish with the rosemary sprigs. Transfer to a wire rack to cool for a few minutes, then serve warm.

CARAMELIZED ONION TART

SERVES 4–6

INGREDIENTS

- 100 G/3½ OZ UNSALTED BUTTER
- 600 G/1 LB 5 OZ ONIONS, THINLY SLICED
- 2 EGGS
- 100 ML/3½ FL OZ DOUBLE CREAM
- 100 G/3½ OZ GRATED GRUYÈRE CHEESE
- 20-CM/8-INCH READY-BAKED PASTRY CASE
- 100 G/3½ OZ PARMESAN CHEESE, COARSELY GRATED
- SALT AND PEPPER

1 Melt the butter in a heavy-based frying pan over a medium heat. Add the onions and cook, stirring frequently to avoid burning, for 30 minutes, or until well-browned and caramelized. Remove the onions from the pan and set aside.

2 Preheat the oven to 190°C/375°F/Gas Mark 5. Beat the eggs in a large bowl, stir in the cream and season to taste with salt and pepper. Add the Gruyère cheese and mix well. Stir in the cooked onions.

3 Pour the egg and onion mixture into the baked pastry case and sprinkle with the Parmesan cheese. Place on a baking tray and bake in the preheated oven for 15–20 minutes until the filling has set and is beginning to brown.

4 Remove from the oven and leave to rest for at least 10 minutes. The tart can be served hot or left to cool to room temperature.

ONION RÖSTI

SERVES 4

INGREDIENTS

- 450 G/1 LB FLOURY POTATOES
- 1 MEDIUM ONION, GRATED
- SALT AND PEPPER
- OIL, FOR SHALLOW FRYING

1 Wash the potatoes, but do not peel them. Place in a large saucepan, cover with water and bring to the boil, covered, over a high heat. Reduce the heat and simmer for about 10 minutes, until the potatoes are just beginning to soften. Be careful not to overcook.

2 Drain the potatoes. Leave to cool, then peel them and grate coarsely. Mix the grated onion with the potatoes. Season the mixture with salt and pepper.

3 Heat the oil in a heavy-based frying pan and spoon in the potato mixture. The rösti can be as thick or as thin as you like, and can be made into one large cake or several individual ones.

4 Cook over a high heat for about 5 minutes, until the bottom is golden, then turn and cook until the second side is brown and crispy. Remove from the heat, drain and serve.

ONION DHAL

SERVES 4

INGREDIENTS

- 100 G/3½ OZ MASOOR DHAL
- 6 TBSP VEGETABLE OIL
- 1 SMALL BUNCH OF SPRING ONIONS, CHOPPED
- 1 TSP FINELY CHOPPED FRESH GINGER
- 1 TSP CRUSHED GARLIC
- ½ TSP CHILLI POWDER
- ½ TSP TURMERIC
- 300 ML/10 FL OZ WATER
- 1 TSP SALT
- 1 FRESH GREEN CHILLI, DESEEDED AND FINELY CHOPPED, AND CHOPPED FRESH CORIANDER LEAVES, TO GARNISH

1 Rinse the lentils thoroughly and set aside until required.

2 Heat the oil in a heavy-based saucepan. Add the spring onions to the pan and fry over a medium heat, stirring frequently, until lightly browned.

3 Reduce the heat and add the ginger, garlic, chilli powder and turmeric. Briefly stir-fry the spring onions with the spices. Add the lentils and stir to blend.

4 Add the water to the lentil mixture, reduce the heat to low and cook for 20–25 minutes.

5 When the lentils are thoroughly cooked and tender, add the salt and stir gently to mix well.

6 Transfer the onion dhal to a serving dish. Garnish with the chopped green chilli and fresh coriander leaves and serve immediately.

LEEK & GOAT'S CHEESE CRÊPES

MAKES 8

INGREDIENTS

- 25 G/1 OZ UNSALTED BUTTER
- ½ TBSP SUNFLOWER OIL
- 200 G/7 OZ LEEKS, HALVED, RINSED AND FINELY SHREDDED
- FRESHLY GRATED NUTMEG, TO TASTE
- 1 TBSP FINELY SNIPPED FRESH CHIVES
- 8 SAVOURY CRÊPES
- 85 G/3 OZ SOFT GOAT'S CHEESE, RIND REMOVED IF NECESSARY, CHOPPED
- SALT AND PEPPER

1 Preheat the oven to 200°C/400°F/ Gas Mark 6. Melt the butter with the oil in a heavy-based saucepan with a lid over a medium–high heat. Add the leeks and stir around so that they are well coated. Stir in salt and pepper to taste. Add a few gratings of nutmeg, then cover the leeks with a sheet of wet greaseproof paper and cover the pan. Reduce the heat to very low and leave the leeks to sweat for 5–7 minutes until very tender, but not brown. Stir in the chives, then taste and adjust the seasoning if necessary.

2 Put 1 crêpe on the work surface and put one-eighth of the leeks on the crêpe, top with one-eighth of the cheese, then fold the crêpe into a square parcel or simply roll it around the filling. Place the stuffed crêpe on a baking tray, then continue to fill and fold or roll the remaining crêpes.

3 Put the baking tray in the oven and bake for 5 minutes, or until the crêpes are hot and the cheese starts to melt. Serve hot.

LEEK & HERB SOUFFLÉS

MAKES 4

INGREDIENTS

- 350 G/12 OZ BABY LEEKS
- 1 TBSP OLIVE OIL
- 125 ML/4 FL OZ VEGETABLE STOCK (SEE PAGE 36)
- 50 G/1¾ OZ WALNUTS
- 2 EGGS, SEPARATED
- 2 TBSP CHOPPED MIXED HERBS
- 2 TBSP NATURAL YOGURT
- SALT AND PEPPER

1 Preheat the oven to 180°C/350°F/Gas Mark 4. Using a sharp knife, finely chop the leeks. Heat the olive oil in a frying pan. Add the leeks and sauté over a medium heat, stirring occasionally, for 2–3 minutes.

2 Add the vegetable stock to the pan, reduce the heat and simmer gently for a further 5 minutes.

3 Place the walnuts in a food processor or blender and process until finely chopped. Add the leek mixture to the nuts and process briefly to form a purée. Transfer to a mixing bowl.

4 Mix together the egg yolks, the herbs and the yogurt until thoroughly combined. Pour the egg mixture into the leek purée. Season with salt and pepper to taste and mix well.

5 In a separate, grease-free mixing bowl, whisk the egg whites until firm peaks form.

6 Fold the egg whites into the leek mixture. Spoon the mixture into 4 lightly greased soufflé dishes and place on a warmed baking tray.

7 Cook in the preheated oven for 35–40 minutes, or until well risen and set. Serve the soufflés immediately.

LEEKS WITH YELLOW BEAN SAUCE

SERVES 4

INGREDIENTS

- 450 G/1 LB LEEKS
- 175 G/6 OZ BABY SWEETCORN COBS
- 6 SPRING ONIONS
- 3 TBSP GROUNDNUT OIL
- 225 G/8 OZ CHINESE LEAVES, SHREDDED
- 4 TBSP YELLOW BEAN SAUCE

1 Using a sharp knife, slice the leeks, halve the baby sweetcorn cobs and thinly slice the spring onions.

2 Heat the groundnut oil in a large, preheated wok or frying pan until it is smoking.

3 Add the leeks, shredded Chinese leaves and baby sweetcorn to the wok.

4 Stir-fry the vegetables over a high heat for about 5 minutes, or until the edges of the vegetables are slightly brown.

5 Add the spring onions to the wok or frying pan, stirring to combine.

6 Add the yellow bean sauce to the wok. Continue to stir-fry the mixture in the wok for a further 2 minutes, or until the yellow bean sauce is heated through and the vegetables are thoroughly coated in the sauce.

7 Transfer the stir-fried vegetables and sauce to warmed serving dishes and serve immediately.

CHILLED GARLIC SOUP

SERVES 4–6

INGREDIENTS

- 500 G/1 LB 2 OZ DAY-OLD COUNTRY-STYLE WHITE BREAD, CRUSTS REMOVED AND TORN
- 5 LARGE GARLIC CLOVES, HALVED
- 125 ML/4 FL OZ EXTRA VIRGIN OLIVE OIL, PLUS A LITTLE EXTRA FOR DRIZZLING
- 4–5 TBSP SHERRY VINEGAR
- 300 G/10½ OZ GROUND ALMONDS
- 1.2 LITRES/2 PINTS WATER, CHILLED
- SALT AND WHITE PEPPER
- SEEDLESS WHITE GRAPES, TO GARNISH

1 Put the bread in a bowl with just enough cold water to cover and leave to soak for 15 minutes. Squeeze the bread dry and transfer it to a food processor.

2 Add the garlic, oil, sherry vinegar to taste, and the ground almonds to the food processor with 250 ml/9 fl oz of the water and process until blended.

3 With the motor running, slowly pour in the remaining water until a smooth soup forms. Taste and add extra sherry vinegar if necessary. Cover and chill for at least 4 hours.

4 To serve, stir well and adjust the seasoning if necessary. Ladle into bowls and float grapes on top with a drizzle of olive oil.

ROAST GARLIC WITH GOAT'S CHEESE

SERVES 4

INGREDIENTS

- 2 GARLIC BULBS, OUTER PAPERY LAYERS REMOVED
- 3 TBSP WATER
- 6 TBSP OLIVE OIL
- 2 FRESH ROSEMARY SPRIGS
- 1 BAY LEAF
- 200 G/7 OZ SOFT GOAT'S CHEESE
- 1 TBSP CHOPPED FRESH MIXED HERBS, SUCH AS PARSLEY AND OREGANO
- 1 BAGUETTE, SLICED
- SALT AND PEPPER
- SALAD LEAVES, TO GARNISH

1 Preheat the oven to 200°C/400°F/Gas Mark 6. Place the garlic in an ovenproof dish. Add the water, half the oil, the rosemary and the bay leaf. Season to taste with salt and pepper. Cover with foil and roast for 30 minutes.

2 Remove the dish from the oven and baste the garlic with the cooking juices. Re-cover and roast for a further 15 minutes, or until tender.

3 Meanwhile, beat the cheese in a bowl until smooth, then beat in the mixed herbs. Heat the remaining oil in a frying pan. Fry the bread on both sides for 3–4 minutes, or until golden brown.

4 Arrange the bread and cheese on serving plates garnished with the salad leaves. Remove the garlic from the oven. Break up the bulbs but do not peel. Divide between the plates and serve immediately. Each diner squeezes the garlic pulp on to the bread and eats it with the cheese.

GARLIC SPAGHETTI

SERVES 4

INGREDIENTS
- 125 ML/4 FL OZ OLIVE OIL
- 3 GARLIC CLOVES, CRUSHED
- 450 G/1 LB FRESH SPAGHETTI
- 3 TBSP ROUGHLY CHOPPED FRESH PARSLEY
- SALT AND PEPPER

1 Reserve 1 tablespoon of the olive oil and heat the remainder in a medium saucepan. Add the garlic and a pinch of salt and cook over a low heat, stirring constantly, until golden brown, then remove the pan from the heat. Do not allow the garlic to burn as this will taint its flavour.

2 Meanwhile, bring a large saucepan of lightly salted water to the boil. Add the spaghetti and remaining olive oil and cook for 2–3 minutes, or until the spaghetti is tender, but still firm to the bite. Drain thoroughly and return to the pan.

3 Add the oil and garlic mixture to the spaghetti and toss to coat thoroughly. Season to taste with pepper, add the parsley and toss well to coat again.

4 Transfer the spaghetti to a warmed serving dish and serve immediately.

NUTS, SEEDS, PULSES & BEANS

Nuts and seeds allow you to incorporate valuable vitamins and 'good' fats into your diet on a daily basis. Protein-rich pulses and beans are staples of the vegetarian kitchen, but the recipes in this chapter show there is more to the vegetarian diet than nut cutlets! These recipes come from vegetarian cultures around the world and include all-time favourites, such as Hummus, along with less-familiar Egyptian Brown Beans and the novel Kidney Bean Risotto.

DIRECTORY OF NUTS & SEEDS

Nuts and seeds are more than just a convenient snack, making a useful and healthy addition to both sweet and savoury vegetarian dishes. Best bought in small quantities from shops that have a high turnover of goods, seeds and nuts – particularly if shelled – can go off if kept for too long after purchase. Stored in an airtight container in a cool, dark place, nuts and seeds should last about three months.

Nuts

Nuts are the fruits of trees, with the exception of peanuts, which grow underground. Although fairly high in fat, it is the beneficial omega-6 type, and they also provide a range of other nutrients, including protein, B vitamins, iron, selenium, vitamin E and zinc. Nuts are available whole, with or without shells, blanched, flaked, chopped, ground or toasted.

Brazil nuts

Brazil nuts have a sweet, milky taste and are particularly rich in omega-6 essential fatty acids. They are often used in muesli-type breakfast cereals or in desserts.

Macadamia nuts

Macadamia nuts have a creamy, rich, buttery flavour and a high fat content. The round nut is usually sold shelled, as the outer casing is extremely hard to crack.

Almonds

Almonds come in two types: bitter and sweet. The former is not recommended raw, but is transformed into a fragrant oil and essence. Sweet almonds are best bought shelled in their skins. You can blanch them yourself in boiling water for a few minutes to remove the skin. However, you can also buy them ready-blanched as well as flaked, toasted and ground, all of which add a richness and pronounced flavour to cakes, desserts and some savoury dishes.

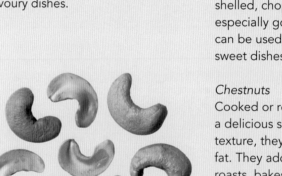

Cashew nuts

Cashew nuts are lower in fat than most other nuts. Their creamy flavour lends itself to roasts, bakes and nut butters, and they add a pleasant crunch to noodle dishes and salads.

Hazelnuts

The versatile hazelnut is sold whole, shelled, chopped and ground, and is especially good roasted. Hazelnuts can be used in both savoury and sweet dishes.

Chestnuts

Cooked or roasted chestnuts have a delicious sweet taste and floury texture, they are also really low in fat. They add substance to stuffings, roasts, bakes and pies. Sweetened chestnut purée is used in desserts.

Pine kernels

The pine kernel is one of the key ingredients in pesto and the tiny cream-coloured nut has a rich, creamy flavour, which is enhanced by toasting. Buy pine kernels in small quantities as their high fat content means that they will go off.

Walnuts
When picked young, walnuts are referred to as 'wet' and have a fresh, milky kernel. However, they are usually bought dried – shelled, chopped or ground – when the nut adopts a slightly bitter flavour.

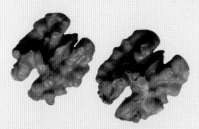

Coconut
Coconut is high in saturated fat, so is best eaten in moderation. Coconut milk and cream add a rich creaminess to sauces, curries, smoothies, desserts and soups. The dense white 'meat' is also made into desiccated or flaked coconut.

Seeds
Albeit tiny, seeds pack a powerful punch when it comes to nutritional status. They are a good source of the antioxidant vitamin E and iron, as well as the essential fatty acid omega-6, which may help in reducing harmful cholesterol levels – all that from a small and unassuming seed!

Sesame seeds
Tiny sesame seeds come in black or white and are used to make a surprising range of products. Ground into a thick paste, they make tahini, the base of hummus and the sweet confection halva; they are also turned into a rich, toasted oil. Their flavour is improved by toasting in a dry frying pan until golden. Sprinkle over salads, noodles, bakes, cakes and breads.

Sunflower seeds
Toasting also improves the flavour of sunflower seeds, but take care not to burn them, as their nutritional content will be affected. The tear-shaped seeds have similar uses to sesame seeds and make a healthy addition to salads, breakfast cereals and flapjacks.

Pumpkin seeds
Pumpkin seeds are one of the few plant foods to contain both omega-3 and omega-6 essential fatty acids and are richer in iron than other seeds. They make a nutritious snack or can be used in much the same way as other seeds.

Poppy seeds
These small black seeds add an attractive decorative look as well as crunch to breads and cakes. They are used in German and Eastern European pastries, strudels and tarts.

Linseeds
Long known for their oil, used to polish wood, these small, golden seeds are also known as flax seeds. Linseeds are one of the few vegetarian sources of omega-3 essential fatty acids and can be sprinkled over breakfast cereals and salads or mixed into breads and pastries.

How to Toast Nuts and Seeds

To remove the papery husk from hazelnuts or almonds, simply put the nuts on a baking tray and heat in a preheated oven at 180°C/350°F/Gas Mark 4 for 5–10 minutes to loosen the skins. Remove from the oven and, when they are cool enough to handle, rub off the skins with a clean tea towel.

Seeds and nuts, such as whole or flaked almonds, are also toasted to enhance their flavour. Smaller quantities of seeds can be toasted in a dry frying pan until they change colour, but for larger amounts, spread them in a single layer on a baking tray and roast in a preheated oven at 180°C/350°F/Gas Mark 4 for 5–7 minutes.

DIRECTORY OF PULSES & BEANS

Lentils, beans and peas are all pulses and are an excellent source of low-fat protein as well as complex carbohydrates, vitamins, minerals and fibre. Their versatility and ability to absorb the flavours of other foods mean that they can form the base of a large number of different dishes.

Although pulses can be kept for up to a year, they do tend to toughen with age. Buy from shops with a high turnover of stock and look for bright, unwrinkled pulses that are not dusty. Store pulses in an airtight container in a cool, dark place and rinse before use. Avoid adding salt to the water when cooking pulses, as this prevents them from softening; instead, season when cooked.

Lentils

Unlike most other pulses, lentils do not require presoaking and are relatively quick to cook. They are sold dried or canned and can be used in a variety of dishes – dahls, burgers, bakes, stews and soups.

Split lentils
Orange-coloured red lentils are the most familiar variety, and because they are 'split', they can be cooked in around 20 minutes, eventually disintegrating into a thick purée. They are ideal for thickening soups and stews, and are used to make the spicy Indian dish, dahl.

Brown lentils
These disc-shaped lentils, sometimes called Continental lentils, have a robust texture and flavour. Available whole, they take longer to cook than red lentils – around 45 minutes – and add substance to stews, stuffings and soups.

Green lentils
Similar to the brown lentil, green lentils have a slightly milder flavour and can be cooked and blended with herbs and garlic to make a nutritious spread. The tiny, dark grey-green Puy lentil is grown in France and is considered superior in flavour to other varieties. They take around 25–30 minutes to cook, but retain their bead-like shape. They

are delicious in warm salads with a vinaigrette dressing and also make a hearty addition to stews.

Dried peas

Unlike lentils, peas are soft when young and need to be dried. Available whole or split, the latter have a sweeter flavour and cook more quickly.

Yellow and green split peas
Yellow and green split peas are interchangeable with red split lentils and are perfect for dahls, soups, casseroles and purées, but they do take slightly longer to cook.

Marrowfat peas
Marrowfat peas are quite large and are used to make the British classic 'mushy' peas. They should be soaked overnight before cooking.

Beans

With the exception of the ubiquitous baked bean, beans are often ignored, yet they are all so versatile, lending themselves to inclusion in pies, bakes, stews, soups, pâtés, dips, burgers, salads and more. What often puts people off is the long soaking time, but canned beans are just as good and incredibly convenient. Just drain and rinse before use.

Chickpeas

Chickpeas resemble shelled hazelnuts and have a nutty flavour and a creamy texture. They are widely used in Indian and Middle Eastern cuisines. In India, they are ground to make the yellow-coloured gram flour, which is used for making fritters and flatbreads.

Flageolet and borlotti

The pretty, pale green flageolet bean has a fresh, delicate taste and soft texture, while the hearty borlotti bean is pinkish-brown in colour with a sweetish flavour and tender texture, and is often used to make Italian bean and pasta soups.

Cannellini

These white, kidney-shaped beans have a soft, creamy texture when cooked. They are equally delicious served warm in salads or puréed to make a tasty, nutritious alternative to mashed potatoes.

Red kidney

Red kidney beans have a soft, 'mealy' texture and retain their colour and shape when cooked. They are used to make Mexican refried beans and are essential to a successful chilli.

Haricot

Haricot beans (navy or Boston beans) are most commonly used for canned baked beans, but the ivory-coloured bean is also good in stews and soups.

Butter and lima

Butter and lima beans are similar in flavour and appearance. These cream-coloured, kidney-shaped beans have a soft, floury texture.

Soya

This versatile bean has all the nutritional properties of animal products, but none of the disadvantages. Soya beans range in colour from creamy yellow through to brown-black and make a healthy addition to soups, casseroles and bakes. The dried beans are very dense and need to be soaked for 12 hours before cooking. Soya beans are used to make tofu, tempeh, meat-replacement mince and chunks, flour, soya milk, soy sauce and miso, as well as a range of sauces, including black bean sauce, yellow bean sauce and hoisin sauce.

Cooking Beans

Once soaked, beans should be drained and rinsed in clean water. Any pulses that have floated to the surface during soaking should be discarded. You need to allow plenty of water for cooking: 1.2 litres/ 2 pints fresh cold water per 450 g/1 lb beans. Bring to the boil over a high heat and boil for 10 minutes, then reduce the heat and simmer until the beans are soft but not mushy, which can take anything from 30 minutes to 2 hours, depending on the type and age of the bean. The beans must always be submerged: top up with boiling water as necessary to keep them covered by about 1 cm/½ inch. The cooking water can be used as a vegetable stock. If you are cooking more than one variety of bean, they need to be soaked and cooked separately, as they will cook at different rates. Remember to add salt only towards the end of cooking.

CHILLED PEA SOUP

SERVES 3–4

INGREDIENTS

- 425 ML/15 FL OZ VEGETABLE STOCK (SEE PAGE 36) OR WATER
- 450 G/1 LB FROZEN PEAS
- 55 G/2 OZ SPRING ONIONS
- 300 ML/10 FL OZ NATURAL YOGURT OR SINGLE CREAM
- SALT AND PEPPER

TO GARNISH

- 2 TBSP CHOPPED FRESH MINT
- 2 TBSP CHOPPED SPRING ONIONS OR CHIVES
- GRATED LEMON RIND

1 Bring the stock to the boil in a large saucepan over a medium heat. Reduce the heat, add the peas and spring onions and simmer for 5 minutes.

2 Cool slightly, then strain twice, making sure that you remove any bits of skin. Pour into a large bowl, season to taste and stir in the yogurt or cream. Cover the bowl with clingfilm and refrigerate for several hours or until thoroughly chilled.

3 To serve, remove from the refrigerator, mix well and ladle into a large tureen or individual soup bowls or mugs. Garnish with the chopped mint and spring onions and the grated lemon rind.

CHICKPEA SOUP

SERVES 6

INGREDIENTS

- 400 G/14 OZ DRIED CHICKPEAS, SOAKED IN COLD WATER OVERNIGHT
- 2 TBSP OLIVE OIL
- 1 ONION, FINELY CHOPPED
- 2 GARLIC CLOVES, FINELY CHOPPED
- 450 G/1 LB SWISS CHARD, TRIMMED AND FINELY SLICED
- 2 FRESH ROSEMARY SPRIGS
- 400 G/14 OZ CANNED CHOPPED TOMATOES
- SALT AND PEPPER
- SLICES OF TOASTED BREAD, TO SERVE

1 Drain the chickpeas and put in a large saucepan. Cover with fresh cold water and bring to the boil, skimming off any foam that rises to the surface with a slotted spoon. Reduce the heat and simmer, uncovered, for 1–1 1/4 hours until tender, topping up with water if necessary.

2 Drain the chickpeas, reserving the cooking water. Season the chickpeas well with salt and pepper. Put two-thirds in a food processor or blender with some of the reserved cooking water and process until smooth, adding more of the cooking water if necessary to achieve a soup consistency. Return to the saucepan.

3 Heat the oil in a medium saucepan, add the onion and garlic and cook over a medium heat, stirring frequently, for 3–4 minutes until the onion is soft. Add the Swiss chard and the rosemary sprigs and

cook, stirring frequently, for 3–4 minutes. Add the tomatoes and cook for a further 5 minutes, or until the tomatoes have broken down to an almost smooth sauce. Remove the rosemary sprigs.

4 Add the Swiss chard and tomato mixture to the chickpea purée and simmer for 2–3 minutes. Taste and adjust the seasoning if necessary.

5 Serve in warmed bowls with the slices of toasted bread on the side.

HUMMUS
TOASTS WITH
OLIVES

SERVES 4

INGREDIENTS

- 400 G/14 OZ CANNED
  CHICKPEAS
- JUICE OF 1 LARGE LEMON
- 6 TBSP TAHINI
- 2 TBSP OLIVE OIL
- 2 GARLIC CLOVES, CRUSHED
- SALT AND PEPPER
- CHOPPED FRESH CORIANDER
  AND BLACK OLIVES,
  TO GARNISH

TOASTS

- 1 CIABATTA LOAF, SLICED
- 2 GARLIC CLOVES, CRUSHED
- 1 TBSP CHOPPED FRESH
  CORIANDER
- 4 TBSP OLIVE OIL

1 To make the hummus, first drain the chickpeas, reserving a little of the liquid. Put the chickpeas and liquid in a food processor and blend, gradually adding the reserved liquid and lemon juice. Blend well after each addition until smooth.

2 Stir in the tahini and all but 1 teaspoon of the olive oil. Add the garlic, season to taste and blend again until smooth.

3 Spoon the hummus into a serving dish. Drizzle the remaining olive oil over the top and garnish with the chopped coriander and olives. Leave to chill in the refrigerator while preparing the toasts.

4 Preheat the grill. Lay the slices of ciabatta on a grill rack in a single layer. Mix the garlic, coriander and olive oil together and drizzle over the bread slices. Cook under the preheated grill for 2–3 minutes until golden brown, turning once. Serve hot with the hummus.

CHICKPEA HOTPOT

SERVES 4

INGREDIENTS

- 225 G/8 OZ DRIED CHICKPEAS, SOAKED IN COLD WATER OVERNIGHT
- 3 TBSP OLIVE OIL
- 1 LARGE ONION, SLICED
- 2 GARLIC CLOVES, FINELY CHOPPED
- 2 LEEKS, SLICED
- 175 G/6 OZ CARROTS, SLICED
- 4 TURNIPS, SLICED
- 4 CELERY STICKS, SLICED
- 115 G/4 OZ BULGUR WHEAT
- 400 G/14 OZ CANNED CHOPPED TOMATOES
- 2 TBSP SNIPPED FRESH CHIVES, PLUS EXTRA TO GARNISH
- SALT AND PEPPER

1 Drain the chickpeas and place in a heavy-based saucepan. Add enough water to cover and bring to the boil. Boil for 15 minutes, then simmer for 1½ hours.

2 Meanwhile, heat the oil in a large saucepan. Add the onion and cook, stirring occasionally, for 5 minutes, until soft. Add the garlic, leeks, carrots, turnips and celery and cook, stirring occasionally, for 5 minutes.

3 Stir in the bulgur, tomatoes and chives, season to taste with salt and pepper and bring to the boil. Spoon the mixture into a heatproof pudding basin and cover with a lid or circle of foil.

4 When the chickpeas have been cooking for 1½ hours, set a steamer over the saucepan. Place the basin in the steamer, cover tightly and cook for 40 minutes. Remove the basin from the steamer, drain the chickpeas, then stir them into the vegetable and bulgur mixture. Transfer the hotpot to a warmed serving dish and serve immediately, garnished with the extra chives.

VEGETABLE & BLACK
BEAN SPRING ROLLS

SERVES 4

INGREDIENTS

- 2 TBSP GROUNDNUT OR VEGETABLE OIL, PLUS EXTRA FOR DEEP-FRYING
- 4 SPRING ONIONS, CUT INTO 5-CM/2-INCH LENGTHS AND SHREDDED LENGTHWAYS
- 2.5-CM/1-INCH PIECE FRESH GINGER, PEELED AND FINELY CHOPPED
- 1 LARGE CARROT, PEELED AND CUT INTO MATCHSTICKS
- 1 RED PEPPER, DESEEDED AND CUT INTO MATCHSTICKS
- 6 TBSP BLACK BEAN SAUCE
- 55 G/2 OZ FRESH BEANSPROUTS
- 200 G/7 OZ CANNED WATER CHESTNUTS, DRAINED AND ROUGHLY CHOPPED
- 5-CM/2-INCH PIECE CUCUMBER, CUT INTO MATCHSTICKS
- 8 X 20-CM/8-INCH SQUARE SPRING ROLL WRAPPERS
- SWEET CHILLI DIPPING SAUCE, TO SERVE (OPTIONAL)

1 Heat the oil in a preheated wok, add the spring onions, ginger, carrot and red pepper and stir-fry over a medium–high heat for 2–3 minutes. Add the black bean sauce, beansprouts, water chestnuts and cucumber and stir-fry for 1–2 minutes. Leave to cool.

2 Remove the spring roll wrappers from the packet, but keep them in a pile, covered with clingfilm, to prevent them drying out. Lay one wrapper on a work surface in front of you in a diamond shape and brush the edges with water. Put a spoonful of the filling near one corner and fold the corner over the filling. Roll over again and then fold the side corners over the filling. Roll up to seal the filling completely. Repeat with the remaining wrappers and filling.

3 Heat the oil for deep-frying in the wok to 180°C/350°F/Gas Mark 4, or until a cube of bread browns in 30 seconds. Add the rolls, in 2–3 batches, and cook for 2–3 minutes until crisp and golden all over. Remove with a slotted spoon, drain on kitchen paper and keep warm while you cook the remaining rolls. Serve with the sweet chilli dipping sauce, if using.

BEAN BURGERS

MAKES 4

INGREDIENTS

- 1 TBSP SUNFLOWER OIL, PLUS EXTRA FOR BRUSHING
- 1 ONION, FINELY CHOPPED
- 1 GARLIC CLOVE, FINELY CHOPPED
- 1 TSP GROUND CORIANDER
- 1 TSP GROUND CUMIN
- 115 G/4 OZ BUTTON MUSHROOMS, FINELY CHOPPED
- 425 G/15 OZ CANNED RED KIDNEY BEANS, DRAINED AND RINSED
- 2 TBSP CHOPPED FRESH FLAT-LEAF PARSLEY
- PLAIN FLOUR, FOR DUSTING
- SALT AND PEPPER
- BURGER BUNS AND SALAD LEAVES, TO SERVE

1 Heat the oil in a heavy-based frying pan over a medium heat. Add the onion and cook, stirring frequently, for 5 minutes, or until soft. Add the garlic, coriander and cumin and cook, stirring, for a further minute. Add the mushrooms and cook, stirring frequently, for 4–5 minutes, until all the liquid has evaporated. Transfer to a bowl.

2 Put the beans in a small bowl and mash with a potato masher. Stir into the mushroom mixture with the parsley and season to taste with salt and pepper.

3 Preheat the grill to medium–high. Divide the mixture equally into 4 portions, dust lightly with flour and shape into flat, round patties. Brush with oil and cook under the grill for 4–5 minutes on each side. Serve in the burger buns with the salad leaves.

BROAD BEANS WITH FETA

SERVES 4–6

INGREDIENTS

- 500 G/1 LB 2 OZ SHELLED BROAD BEANS
- 4 TBSP EXTRA VIRGIN OLIVE OIL
- 1 TBSP LEMON JUICE
- 1 TBSP FINELY CHOPPED FRESH DILL, PLUS EXTRA TO GARNISH
- 55 G/2 OZ FETA CHEESE, DRAINED AND DICED
- SALT AND PEPPER

1 Bring a large saucepan of lightly salted water to the boil. Add the broad beans and cook for about 2 minutes, until tender. Drain thoroughly and set aside.

2 When the beans are cool enough to handle, remove and discard the outer skins to reveal the bright green beans underneath. Put the peeled beans in a serving bowl.

3 Combine the olive oil and lemon juice, then season to taste with salt and pepper. Pour the dressing over the warm beans, add the dill and stir gently. Adjust the seasoning, if necessary.

4 If serving hot, add the cheese, toss gently and sprinkle with the extra dill, then serve immediately. Alternatively, set aside the beans in their dressing to cool and then chill until required.

5 To serve cold, remove from the refrigerator 10 minutes before serving to bring to room temperature. Taste and adjust the seasoning, if necessary, then sprinkle with the cheese and extra dill.

SAUCY BORLOTTI BEANS

SERVES 4–6

INGREDIENTS

- 600 G/1 LB 5 OZ FRESH BORLOTTI BEANS
- 4 LARGE LEAVES FRESH SAGE, TORN
- 1 TBSP OLIVE OIL
- 1 LARGE ONION, THINLY SLICED
- 300 ML/10 FL OZ TOMATO SAUCE (SEE PAGE 37)
- SALT AND PEPPER

1 Shell the beans. Bring a large saucepan of water to the boil, add the beans and torn sage leaves, bring back to the boil and simmer for about 12 minutes or until the beans are tender. Drain and set aside.

2 Heat the olive oil in a large, heavy-based frying pan over a medium heat. Add the onion and cook, stirring occasionally, for about 5 minutes until softened and translucent, but not browned. Stir the Tomato Sauce into the pan with the cooked borlotti beans and the torn sage leaves.

3 Increase the heat and bring to the boil, stirring. Reduce the heat, partially cover and simmer for about 10 minutes, or until the sauce has reduced slightly.

4 Adjust the seasoning, transfer to a serving bowl and serve hot.

EGYPTIAN BROWN BEANS

SERVES 4–6 AS PART OF A MEZE

INGREDIENTS

- 300 G/10½ OZ DRIED FUL MEDAMES, RINSED AND SOAKED IN COLD WATER FOR AT LEAST 12 HOURS WITH 1 TBSP BICARBONATE OF SODA
- 2 TBSP OLIVE OIL
- 1 ONION, FINELY CHOPPED
- 1 LARGE GARLIC CLOVE, CRUSHED TO A PASTE WITH 1 TSP SALT
- 1 LARGE TOMATO, DESEEDED AND FINELY CHOPPED
- SALT AND PEPPER

TO SERVE

- 1 FRESH RED CHILLI, DESEEDED AND FINELY CHOPPED, OR ½ TSP DRIED CHILLI FLAKES (OPTIONAL)
- 1 LEMON, HALVED
- EXTRA VIRGIN OLIVE OIL
- WARMED ARAB FLATBREAD OR PITTA BREAD

1 Drain the beans and rinse well. Put in a saucepan with fresh cold water to cover and bring to the boil. Boil rapidly for 10 minutes, skimming off any foam that rises to the surface. Reduce the heat to low, cover and simmer for at least 2 hours, or until tender enough to be easily mashed between your fingers, topping up the water as necessary. Drain the beans, reserving the cooking water.

2 Heat the olive oil in a large frying pan. Add the onion and cook over a medium heat, stirring frequently, for 5 minutes, or until very soft and golden but not brown. Use a slotted spoon to transfer half the beans to the pan, stir and mash into the onion. Add the remaining beans and the tomato and heat through. Add salt and pepper to taste. If the mixture is too thick to be scooped up with flat bread, slowly add some of the reserved cooking water until you reach the desired consistency.

3 Spoon the beans into a serving bowl. Scatter the chilli over the top, if using, then squeeze over the juice from the lemon halves to taste and drizzle with the extra virgin olive oil. Serve with the bread for scooping up the beans.

KIDNEY BEAN RISOTTO

SERVES 4

INGREDIENTS

- 4 TBSP OLIVE OIL
- 1 ONION, CHOPPED
- 2 GARLIC CLOVES, FINELY CHOPPED
- 175 G/6 OZ BROWN RICE
- 600 ML/1 PINT VEGETABLE STOCK (SEE PAGE 36)
- 1 RED PEPPER, DESEEDED AND CHOPPED
- 2 CELERY STICKS, SLICED
- 225 G/8 OZ CHESTNUT MUSHROOMS, THINLY SLICED
- 425 G/15 OZ CANNED RED KIDNEY BEANS, DRAINED AND RINSED
- 3 TBSP CHOPPED FRESH PARSLEY, PLUS EXTRA TO GARNISH
- 55 G/2 OZ CASHEW NUTS
- SALT AND PEPPER

1 Heat half the oil in a large, heavy-based saucepan. Add the onion and cook, stirring occasionally, for 5 minutes, or until soft. Add half the garlic and cook, stirring frequently, for 2 minutes, then add the rice and stir for 1 minute, or until the grains are thoroughly coated with the oil. Add the stock and a pinch of salt and bring to the boil, stirring constantly. Reduce the heat, cover and simmer for 35–40 minutes, or until all the liquid has been absorbed.

2 Meanwhile, heat the remaining oil in a heavy-based frying pan. Add the red pepper and celery and cook, stirring frequently, for 5 minutes. Add the mushrooms and the remaining garlic and cook, stirring frequently, for 4–5 minutes.

3 Stir the rice into the frying pan. Add the beans, parsley and cashew nuts. Season to taste and cook, stirring constantly, until piping hot. Transfer to a warmed serving dish, sprinkle with the extra parsley and serve.

GREEN BEAN SALAD
WITH FETA

SERVES 4

INGREDIENTS

- 350 G/12 OZ GREEN BEANS, TRIMMED
- 1 RED ONION, CHOPPED
- 3–4 TBSP CHOPPED FRESH CORIANDER
- 2 RADISHES, THINLY SLICED
- 75 G/2¾ OZ FETA CHEESE, CRUMBLED
- 1 TSP CHOPPED FRESH OREGANO OR ½ TSP DRIED OREGANO
- 2 TBSP RED WINE OR FRUIT VINEGAR
- 5 TBSP EXTRA VIRGIN OLIVE OIL
- 3 RIPE TOMATOES, CUT INTO WEDGES
- PEPPER

1 Bring about 5 cm/2 inches water to the boil in the base of a steamer or in a medium saucepan. Add the beans to the top of the steamer or place them in a metal colander set over the pan of water. Cover and steam for about 5 minutes, until just tender.

2 Transfer the beans to a bowl and add the onion, coriander, radishes and cheese.

3 Sprinkle the oregano over the salad, then grind pepper over to taste. Whisk the vinegar and olive oil together and pour over the salad. Toss gently to mix well.

4 Transfer to a serving platter, add the tomato wedges and serve at once or chill until ready to serve.

SESAME HOT NOODLES

SERVES 4

INGREDIENTS

- 500 G/18 OZ DRIED MEDIUM EGG NOODLES
- 3 TBSP SUNFLOWER OIL
- 2 TBSP SESAME OIL
- 1 GARLIC CLOVE, CRUSHED
- 1 TBSP SMOOTH PEANUT BUTTER
- 1 SMALL GREEN CHILLI, DESEEDED AND VERY FINELY CHOPPED
- 3 TBSP TOASTED SESAME SEEDS
- 4 TBSP LIGHT SOY SAUCE
- ½ TBSP LIME JUICE
- 4 TBSP CHOPPED FRESH CORIANDER
- SALT AND PEPPER

1. Place the noodles in a large saucepan of boiling water, then immediately remove from the heat. Cover and leave to stand for 6 minutes, stirring once halfway through the time. At the end of 6 minutes the noodles will be perfectly cooked. Alternatively, cook the noodles following the packet instructions.

2. Meanwhile, make the dressing. Mix together the sunflower oil, sesame oil, crushed garlic and peanut butter in a mixing bowl until smooth.

3. Add the chopped green chilli, sesame seeds and soy sauce to the bowl. Add the lime juice, according to taste, and mix well. Season to taste with salt and pepper.

4. Drain the noodles thoroughly then place in a heated serving bowl.

5. Add the dressing and the chopped coriander to the noodles and toss well to mix. Serve hot.

PASTA WITH PESTO

SERVES 4

INGREDIENTS
- 450 G/1 LB DRIED TAGLIATELLE
- SALT
- FRESH BASIL LEAVES, TO GARNISH

PESTO
- 2 GARLIC CLOVES
- 25 G/1 OZ PINE KERNELS
- 115 G/4 OZ FRESH BASIL LEAVES
- 55 G/2 OZ FRESHLY GRATED PARMESAN CHEESE
- 125 ML/4 FL OZ OLIVE OIL
- SALT

1 To make the pesto, put the garlic, pine kernels, a large pinch of salt and the basil into a mortar and pound to a paste with a pestle. Transfer to a bowl and gradually work in the Parmesan cheese with a wooden spoon, followed by the olive oil to make a thick, creamy sauce. Taste and adjust the seasoning if necessary.

2 Alternatively, put the garlic, pine kernels and a large pinch of salt into a blender or food processor and process briefly. Add the basil leaves and process to a paste. With the motor still running, gradually add the olive oil. Scrape into a bowl and beat in the cheese. Season to taste with salt.

3 Bring a large saucepan of lightly salted water to the boil. Add the pasta, return to the boil and cook for 8–10 minutes, or until tender but still firm to the bite. Drain well, return to the saucepan and toss with half the pesto, then divide between warmed serving plates and top with the remaining pesto. Garnish with the basil leaves and serve.

NUTTY STILTON ROAST

SERVES 6–8

INGREDIENTS

- 2 TBSP VIRGIN OLIVE OIL, PLUS EXTRA FOR OILING
- 2 ONIONS
- 3–5 GARLIC CLOVES, CRUSHED
- 2 CELERY STALKS, FINELY SLICED
- 175 G/6 OZ COOKED AND PEELED CHESTNUTS
- 175 G/6 OZ MIXED CHOPPED NUTS
- 55 G/2 OZ GROUND ALMONDS
- 55 G/2 OZ FRESH WHOLEMEAL BREADCRUMBS
- 225 G/8 OZ STILTON CHEESE, CRUMBLED
- 1 TBSP CHOPPED FRESH BASIL, PLUS EXTRA SPRIGS TO GARNISH
- 1 EGG, BEATEN
- SALT AND PEPPER
- 1 RED PEPPER, SKINNED, DESEEDED AND CUT INTO THIN WEDGES
- 1 COURGETTE, ABOUT 115 G/ 4 OZ, CUT INTO WEDGES
- CHERRY TOMATOES, TO GARNISH
- TOMATO SAUCE (SEE PAGE 37) AND LIGHTLY COOKED GREEN VEGETABLES, TO SERVE

1 Preheat the oven to 180°C/350°F/Gas Mark 4. Lightly oil a 900-g/2-lb loaf tin.

2 Finely chop one of the onions. Heat 1 tablespoon of the oil in a frying pan over a medium heat, add the chopped onion, 1–2 of the garlic cloves and the celery and cook for 5 minutes, stirring occasionally.

3 Remove from the pan, drain through a sieve or colander and transfer to a food processor with the nuts, breadcrumbs, half the cheese and the basil. Using the pulse button, blend the ingredients together, then slowly blend in the egg to form a stiff mixture. Season to taste with salt and pepper.

4 Cut the remaining onion into thin wedges. Heat the remaining oil in a frying pan over a medium heat, add the onion, remaining garlic, red pepper and courgette and cook for 5 minutes, stirring frequently. Remove from the pan, add salt and pepper to taste and drain through a sieve or colander.

5 Place half the nut mixture in the prepared tin and smooth the surface. Arrange the onion and pepper mixture on top and crumble over the remaining cheese. Top with the remaining nut mixture and press down firmly. Cover with foil.

6 Bake in the preheated oven for 45 minutes. Remove the foil and bake for a further 25–35 minutes, or until cooked and firm to the touch.

7 Remove from the oven and leave to cool for 5 minutes before inverting on to a warmed serving platter. Serve with a little of the Tomato Sauce drizzled over the top, garnished with basil sprigs and cherry tomatoes, accompanied by vegetables.

CASHEW NUT PAELLA

SERVES 4

INGREDIENTS

- 2 TBSP OLIVE OIL
- 1 TBSP BUTTER
- 1 RED ONION, CHOPPED
- 150 G/5½ OZ ARBORIO RICE
- 1 TSP TURMERIC
- 1 TSP GROUND CUMIN
- ½ TSP CHILLI POWDER
- 3 GARLIC CLOVES, CRUSHED
- 1 FRESH GREEN CHILLI, DESEEDED AND SLICED
- 1 GREEN PEPPER, DESEEDED AND DICED
- 1 RED PEPPER, DESEEDED AND DICED
- 85 G/3 OZ BABY SWEETCORN COBS, HALVED LENGTHWAYS
- 2 TBSP STONED BLACK OLIVES
- 1 LARGE TOMATO, DESEEDED AND DICED
- 450 ML/16 FL OZ VEGETABLE STOCK
- 85 G/3 OZ UNSALTED CASHEW NUTS
- 55 G/2 OZ FROZEN PEAS
- 2 TBSP CHOPPED FRESH PARSLEY
- PINCH OF CAYENNE PEPPER
- SALT AND PEPPER
- FRESH HERBS, TO GARNISH

1 Heat the olive oil and butter in a large frying pan or paella pan until the butter has melted.

2 Add the onion and cook over a medium heat, stirring constantly, for 2–3 minutes until softened.

3 Stir in the rice, turmeric, cumin, chilli powder, garlic, sliced chilli, green and red peppers, corn cobs, olives and tomato and cook over a medium heat, stirring occasionally, for 1–2 minutes.

4 Pour in the stock and bring the mixture to the boil. Reduce the heat and cook gently, stirring constantly,
for a further 20 minutes.

5 Add the cashew nuts and peas and continue to cook, stirring occasionally, for a further 5 minutes. Season to taste with salt and pepper and add the chopped fresh parsley and a pinch of cayenne pepper. Transfer the paella to warm serving plates, garnish with fresh herbs and serve immediately.

STILTON & WALNUT TARTLETS

SERVES 4

INGREDIENTS

WALNUT PASTRY
- 225 G/8 OZ PLAIN FLOUR, PLUS EXTRA FOR DUSTING
- PINCH OF CELERY SALT
- 100 G/3½ OZ COLD BUTTER, DICED, PLUS EXTRA FOR GREASING
- 25 G/1 OZ WALNUT HALVES, CHOPPED
- ICE-COLD WATER

FILLING
- 25 G/1 OZ BUTTER
- 2 CELERY STICKS, FINELY CHOPPED
- 1 SMALL LEEK, FINELY CHOPPED
- 200 ML/7 FL OZ DOUBLE CREAM, PLUS 2 TBSP
- 200 G/7 OZ STILTON CHEESE
- 3 EGG YOLKS
- SALT AND PEPPER

1 Lightly grease a 12-hole muffin tin. Sift the flour with the celery salt into a food processor, add the butter and process until the mixture resembles breadcrumbs. Tip into a large bowl and add the walnuts and a little cold water, just enough to bring the dough together. Turn out on to a lightly floured work surface and cut the dough in half. Roll out the first piece and cut out six 9-cm/3½-inch rounds. Roll out each round to a diameter of 12 cm/4½ inches and use to line the muffin tin. Repeat with the remaining dough. Line each hole with baking paper and fill with baking beans. Chill in the refrigerator for 30 minutes. Meanwhile, preheat the oven to 200°C/400°F/Gas Mark 6.

2 Bake the tartlet cases for 10 minutes. Remove from the oven, then take out the paper and beans.

3 To make the filling, melt the butter in a frying pan over a medium–low heat, add the celery and leek and cook, stirring occasionally, for 15 minutes, until very soft. Add the 2 tablespoons of cream, crumble in the cheese and mix well. Season to taste with salt and pepper. Put the remaining cream in a saucepan and bring to simmering point. Pour on to the egg yolks in a heatproof bowl, stirring constantly. Mix in the cheese mixture and spoon into the tartlet cases. Bake for 10 minutes, then turn the tin around in the oven and bake for a further 5 minutes. Leave the tartlets to cool in the tin for 5 minutes and serve.

BRASSICAS &
LEAVES

There isn't any need to forgo the pleasures of eating salads in the winter just because soft, delicate leaves don't appeal at that time of year. This chapter has plenty of ideas for super salads that hit the spot all year round and for how to bake, purée and stir-fry members of the often-neglected cabbage family into dishes family and friends will enjoy. Be sure to make enough for seconds all round!

DIRECTORY OF BRASSICAS & LEAVES

This large group of vegetables includes many old familiars, such as cauliflower, cabbage and broccoli, as well as more exotic examples, such as pak choi. In the past, these vegetables have suffered greatly from overcooking and their associations with institutional cooking, but, properly cooked, they are delicious and have enormous nutritional value.

Brassicas

This large and varied group of vegetables boasts an extraordinary range of health properties and should form a regular part of our diet – at least 3–4 times a week. They provide numerous phytochemicals, a group of compounds that have been found to provide an anti-carcinogenic cocktail and play a crucial role in fighting disease by stimulating the body's defences. Brassicas are best cooked lightly. Overcooking them not only destroys many of the nutrients, but also affects their flavour. Steaming or stir-frying are preferable to boiling for this reason. Some people dislike brassicas because of their slight bitterness, so serving them in a cream or cheese sauce may help. They also work well in Asian dishes.

Broccoli

There are two types of broccoli: the slender-stemmed purple sprouting type is the original type of broccoli, with long stalks and small purple flower heads. The leaves, stalks and head are all edible. The readily available calabrese has a tightly budded top and thick stalk. Choose broccoli with dark green or purple florets and avoid any with signs of yellowing or a wilted stalk. When serving broccoli, do not forget the stalk, which is also nutritious. The stalk can be served raw, grated into salads or cut into crudités.

Cabbage

When lightly cooked or served shredded in a salad, cabbage is delicious. Cabbages range from the crinkly-leaved Savoy, which is ideal for stuffing, to the smooth and firm white and red varieties. Add a little vinegar to the cooking water when

preparing red cabbage to preserve its colour. Chinese cabbage has a more delicate flavour and is good in salads or stir-fries.

Cauliflower

Cauliflower comes in many varieties, ranging from white to pale green and purple, but all should be encased in green outer leaves, as these protect the more delicate florets.

Brussels sprouts

Reminiscent of Christmas, Brussels sprouts are like miniature cabbages and have a strong, nutty flavour. Sprouts are sweeter when picked after the first frost. They are best cooked very lightly or, better still, stir-fried.

Leafy greens

Research into the health benefits of leafy greens shows that by eating spinach, chard, pak choi, spring greens and spinach beet on a regular basis, you may protect yourself against certain forms of cancer. Leafy vegetables are tastiest served steamed or stir-fried and go particularly well with Asian dishes that include garlic, ginger, chilli and soy sauce.

Spinach
Spinach does provide iron, but not in such rich amounts as was once believed and in a form that is not easy to assimilate. However, combining spinach with vitamin C-rich foods increases absorption. Nutritionally, it is most beneficial when eaten raw and the young leaves are best for this.

Chard
Like spinach, chard should have dark green leaves and a white or red stem. As the stem takes longer to cook than the leaves, it is best sliced and cooked slightly before the leaves are added. Spinach beet is similar to Swiss chard and has a mild flavour. Spring greens are full of flavour and nutrients and should have dark green leaves.

Pak choi
The most typical pak choi features dark green leaves at the top of thick, white, upright stalks. It has a mild flavour, which makes it popular with children, and makes a delightful addition to stir-fries, soups, noodle dishes and salads. The stalk takes slightly longer to cook than the leaves.

Salad leaves

Salad leaves come in a huge variety of shapes, textures, colours and flavours, from the bitter-tasting endive to peppery watercress and delicate butterhead lettuce. Convenient bags of mixed salad leaves allow you to sample a wide range of different types, although they do not tend to last as long as the individually packed types.

Lettuces
Cos and Webbs have firm, crisp leaves, while Little Gem is a smaller, sweeter version of cos. The pretty frilly leaves of lollo rosso are green at the base and a deep red around the edge. Equally attractive is the oakleaf lettuce. Nutritionally, lettuce is best eaten raw, with the darker outer leaves containing more nutrients than the pale-coloured inner. However, it can also be braised, steamed and turned into soups.

Other salad leaves
Cress, mizuna, rocket and watercress have a strong, distinctive flavour and will enliven any salad. Escarole, frisée and radicchio are slightly bitter in flavour and are best used in moderation as they can easily dominate a salad.

BROCCOLI & CHEESE SOUP

SERVES 6

INGREDIENTS

- 25 G/1 OZ BUTTER
- 1 ONION, CHOPPED
- 2 TSP CHOPPED FRESH TARRAGON, PLUS EXTRA TO GARNISH
- 450 G/1 LB POTATOES, PEELED AND GRATED
- 1.7 LITRES/3 PINTS VEGETABLE STOCK (SEE PAGE 36)
- 700 G/1 LB 9 OZ BROCCOLI, CUT INTO SMALL FLORETS
- 175 G/6 OZ CHEDDAR CHEESE
- 1 TBSP CHOPPED FRESH PARSLEY
- SALT AND PEPPER

1 Melt the butter in a large, heavy-based saucepan. Add the onion and cook, stirring occasionally, for 5 minutes, until soft. Add the freshly chopped tarragon to the saucepan with the potatoes, season to taste and mix well. Pour in just enough of the stock to cover and bring to the boil. Reduce the heat, cover and simmer for 10 minutes.

2 Meanwhile, bring the remaining stock to the boil in another saucepan. Add the broccoli and cook for 6–8 minutes, until just tender.

3 Remove both pans from the heat, leave to cool slightly, then ladle the contents of both into a blender or food processor. Process until smooth, then pour the mixture into a clean saucepan. Grate the cheese, stir into the pan with the parsley and heat gently to warm through, but do not allow the soup to boil. Ladle into warmed soup bowls, garnish with tarragon and serve immediately.

TRADITIONAL BEAN & CABBAGE SOUP

SERVES 6

INGREDIENTS

- 200 G/7 OZ DRIED CANNELLINI BEANS, SOAKED IN COLD WATER OVERNIGHT
- 3 TBSP OLIVE OIL
- 2 RED ONIONS, ROUGHLY CHOPPED
- 4 CARROTS, PEELED AND SLICED
- 4 CELERY STICKS, ROUGHLY CHOPPED
- 4 GARLIC CLOVES, ROUGHLY CHOPPED
- 600 ML/1 PINT WATER OR VEGETABLE STOCK (SEE PAGE 36)
- 400 G/14 OZ CANNED CHOPPED TOMATOES
- 2 TBSP CHOPPED FRESH FLAT-LEAF PARSLEY
- 500 G/1 LB 2 OZ CAVOLO NERO, TRIMMED AND FINELY SLICED
- 1 SMALL 2-DAY-OLD CIABATTA LOAF, TORN INTO SMALL PIECES
- SALT AND PEPPER
- EXTRA VIRGIN OLIVE OIL, TO SERVE

1 Drain the beans and put in a large saucepan. Cover with fresh cold water and bring to the boil, skimming off any foam that rises to the surface with a slotted spoon. Reduce the heat and simmer, uncovered, for 1–1¹/₂ hours until tender, topping up with water if required.

2 Meanwhile, heat the olive oil in a large saucepan, add the onions, carrots and celery and cook over a medium heat, stirring frequently, for 10–15 minutes until soft. Add the garlic and cook, stirring, for 1–2 minutes.

3 Drain the beans, reserving the cooking water, and add half the beans to the vegetable mixture. Pour in the measured water and tomatoes, add the parsley and season well with salt and pepper. Bring to a simmer and cook, uncovered and stirring occasionally, for 30 minutes. Add the cavolo nero and cook, stirring occasionally, for a further 15 minutes.

4 Put the remaining beans in a food processor or blender with some of the reserved cooking water and process until smooth. Add to the soup. Stir in the bread. The soup should be thick, but add more of the reserved cooking water to thin if necessary. Continue to cook until heated through.

5 Serve hot with a drizzle of extra virgin olive oil.

SPINACH & FETA PASTRY TRIANGLES

MAKES 12

INGREDIENTS

- 12 SHEETS FILO PASTRY, ABOUT 30 X 23 CM/12 X 9 INCHES EACH, THAWED, IF FROZEN
- ABOUT 200 G/7 OZ BUTTER, MELTED AND COOLED

FILLING

- 250 G/9 OZ BABY SPINACH LEAVES, COOKED
- 2 TBSP OLIVE OIL, PLUS EXTRA FOR OILING
- 4 SPRING ONIONS, FINELY CHOPPED
- 1 SMALL GARLIC CLOVE, CRUSHED
- 2 TBSP CHOPPED FRESH DILL
- 125 G/4½ OZ FETA CHEESE (DRAINED WEIGHT), CRUMBLED
- 1 LARGE EGG, BEATEN
- ¼ TSP FRESHLY GRATED NUTMEG
- 2 TBSP PINE KERNELS, TOASTED (OPTIONAL)
- 2 TBSP RAISINS (OPTIONAL)
- SALT (OPTIONAL) AND PEPPER

1 To make the filling, put the spinach in a large mixing bowl and set aside. Heat the oil in a frying pan. Add the spring onions and cook over a medium heat, stirring frequently, for 1 minute. Add the garlic and cook, stirring, for a further 1–2 minutes, or until the spring onions are soft. Add to the spinach with the dill, feta cheese, egg, nutmeg, pine kernels and raisins, if using, and pepper to taste – the texture will be very runny.

2 Preheat the oven to 190°C/375°F/Gas Mark 5. Lightly brush 1 or 2 baking sheets with oil. Lay one sheet of filo pastry on a work surface and brush all over with melted butter. Top with another sheet of filo and brush with butter, then add a third and again brush with butter. Cut the 3 layers into long strips 7.5 cm/3 inches wide. Cut a total of 12 sets of strips. Arrange one set of strips on the work surface vertically in front of you. Keep the filo you are not using tightly covered with damp (not wet) kitchen paper so that it does not dry out.

3 Stir the filling and put 1 tablespoon in the bottom left-hand corner of the strip, about 5 mm/¼ inch from the short edge. Gently lift the corner over the filling to form a triangle so that the bottom edge now runs along the right-hand side. Fold the triangle upwards, then to the left so that the open edges are across the top and the filling is enclosed. Continue folding the triangle from side to side until you reach the top. Dab the small strip of pastry at the top with water and fold over the triangle to seal. Transfer to the prepared baking sheet, seam side down, and brush with melted butter. Repeat with the remaining sets of filo strips.

4 Bake in the preheated oven for 12–15 minutes, or until golden brown and crisp. Serve hot or warm.

CAULIFLOWER, BROCCOLI & CASHEW NUT SALAD

SERVES 4

INGREDIENTS

- 2 TBSP GROUNDNUT OR VEGETABLE OIL
- 2 RED ONIONS, CUT INTO WEDGES
- 1 SMALL HEAD CAULIFLOWER, CUT INTO FLORETS
- 1 SMALL HEAD BROCCOLI, CUT INTO FLORETS
- 2 TBSP READY-MADE YELLOW CURRY PASTE OR RED CURRY PASTE
- 400 ML/14 FL OZ CANNED COCONUT MILK
- 1 TSP SOY SAUCE
- 1 TSP PALM SUGAR
- 1 TSP SALT
- 85 G/3 OZ UNSALTED CASHEW NUTS
- HANDFUL OF FRESH CORIANDER, CHOPPED, PLUS EXTRA SPRIGS, TORN, TO GARNISH

1 Heat the oil in a preheated wok, add the onions and stir-fry over a medium–high heat for 3–4 minutes, until starting to brown. Add the cauliflower and broccoli and stir-fry for 1–2 minutes. Stir in the curry paste and stir-fry for 30 seconds, then add the coconut milk, sauce, sugar and salt. Bring gently to the boil, stirring occasionally, then reduce the heat and simmer gently for 3–4 minutes, until the vegetables are almost tender.

2 Meanwhile, heat a separate dry frying pan until hot, add the cashew nuts and cook, shaking the pan frequently, for 2–3 minutes, until lightly browned. Add to the stir-fry with the coriander, stir well and serve immediately, garnished with the torn coriander sprigs.

SPINACH LASAGNE

SERVES 4

INGREDIENTS

- 115 G/4 OZ BUTTER, PLUS EXTRA FOR GREASING
- 2 GARLIC CLOVES, FINELY CHOPPED
- 115 G/4 OZ SHALLOTS, FINELY CHOPPED
- 225 G/8 OZ WILD MUSHROOMS, SUCH AS CHANTERELLES, SLICED
- 450 G/1 LB SPINACH, COOKED, DRAINED AND FINELY CHOPPED
- 225 G/8 OZ CHEDDAR CHEESE, GRATED
- ¼ TSP FRESHLY GRATED NUTMEG
- 1 TSP CHOPPED FRESH BASIL
- 6 TBSP PLAIN FLOUR
- 600 ML/1 PINT HOT MILK
- 55 G/2 OZ CHESHIRE CHEESE, GRATED
- 8 SHEETS OF LASAGNA (THE NO-NEED-TO-PRE-COOK VARIETY)
- SALT AND PEPPER

1 Lightly grease a large, fairly deep, rectangular or square ovenproof dish with a little butter.

2 Melt 55 g/2 oz of the butter in a large frying pan. Add the garlic, shallots and mushrooms and fry over a low heat, stirring occasionally, for 3 minutes.

3 Stir in the spinach, Cheddar cheese, nutmeg and basil. Season with salt and pepper to taste, remove from the heat and set aside.

4 Melt the remaining butter in a saucepan over a low heat. Add the flour and cook over a low heat, stirring constantly, for 1 minute. Gradually stir in the hot milk, whisking constantly until smooth and thick. Remove the pan from the heat, stir in 25 g/1 oz of the Cheshire cheese and season to taste with salt and pepper.

5 Spread half the mushroom and spinach mixture over the base of the prepared dish. Cover with half the lasagne sheets and then with half of the cheese sauce. Repeat the layers and then sprinkle the remaining grated Cheshire cheese over the top.

6 Bake in a preheated oven, 200°C/ 400°F/Gas Mark 6, for 30 minutes, or until golden brown. Serve hot.

STUFFED CABBAGE ROLLS

SERVES 4

INGREDIENTS

- 8 LARGE OR 12 MEDIUM GREEN CABBAGE LEAVES
- 1 LITRE/1¾ PINTS WATER
- 100 G/3½ OZ PEARL BARLEY
- 2 TBSP CHOPPED FRESH PARSLEY
- 2 GARLIC CLOVES, COARSELY CHOPPED
- 800 G/1 LB 12 OZ CANNED CHOPPED TOMATOES
- 4 TBSP RED WINE VINEGAR
- 1 TBSP SUNFLOWER OR CORN OIL, PLUS EXTRA FOR BRUSHING
- 2 COURGETTES, DICED
- 3 SPRING ONIONS, SLICED
- 2 TBSP BROWN SUGAR
- SALT AND PEPPER

1 Cut out the thick stems from the cabbage leaves. Bring a large saucepan of water to the boil, add the cabbage leaves and blanch for 1 minute. Drain the leaves well and spread out to dry. Bring the measured water to the boil in a large saucepan. Add the barley and half the chopped parsley, cover and simmer for about 45 minutes, until the liquid has been absorbed.

2 Meanwhile, put the garlic, half the tomatoes and the vinegar in a blender or food processor and process to a smooth purée. Scrape into a bowl and set aside. Heat the oil in a large frying pan. Add the courgettes and the remaining parsley and cook, stirring frequently, for 3 minutes. Add the spring onions and cook briefly, then add the tomato purée mixture. Cook for about 10 minutes, until thickened, then transfer to a large bowl.

3 Add the cooked barley to the bowl, season to taste with salt and pepper and stir well. Lightly brush an ovenproof dish with oil. Place a spoonful of the barley mixture at the stem end of a cabbage leaf. Roll up, tucking in the sides, and place, seam side down, in the dish. Stuff and roll the remaining cabbage leaves in the same way, placing them in the dish in a single layer. Sprinkle the brown sugar over the cabbage rolls and pour the remaining tomatoes, with their can juices, on top. Cover with foil and bake in a preheated oven, 190°C/375°F/Gas Mark 5, for 30 minutes, or until tender. Serve straight from the dish.

CAULIFLOWER & BROCCOLI FLAN

SERVES 4

INGREDIENTS

PASTRY

- 175 G/6 OZ PLAIN FLOUR, PLUS EXTRA FOR DUSTING
- PINCH OF SALT
- ¼ TSP PAPRIKA
- 1 TSP DRIED THYME
- 6 TBSP MARGARINE
- 3 TBSP WATER

FILLING

- 100 G/3½ OZ CAULIFLOWER FLORETS
- 100 G/3½ OZ BROCCOLI FLORETS
- 1 ONION, CUT INTO 8 WEDGES
- 2 TBSP BUTTER OR MARGARINE
- 1 TBSP PLAIN FLOUR
- 6 TBSP VEGETABLE STOCK (SEE PAGE 36)
- 125 ML/4 FL OZ MILK
- 85 G/3 OZ CHEDDAR CHEESE, GRATED
- SALT AND PEPPER
- PAPRIKA, TO GARNISH

1 To make the pastry, sift the flour and salt into a bowl. Add the paprika and thyme and rub in the margarine. Stir in the water and bind to form a dough.

2 Roll out the pastry on a floured surface and use to line an 18-cm/7-inch loose-based flan tin. Prick the base with a fork and line with baking paper. Fill with baking beans and bake in a preheated oven, 190°C/375°F/Gas Mark 5, for 15 minutes. Remove the paper and beans and return the pastry case to the oven for 5 minutes.

3 To make the filling, bring a large saucepan of lightly salted water to the boil, add the cauliflower, broccoli and onion and cook for 10–12 minutes, until tender. Drain and reserve.

4 Melt the butter in a saucepan. Add the flour and cook, stirring constantly, for 1 minute. Remove from the heat, stir in the stock and milk and return to the heat. Bring to the boil, stirring constantly, and add 55 g/2 oz of the cheese. Season to taste with salt and pepper.

5 Spoon the cauliflower, broccoli and onion into the pastry case. Pour over the sauce and sprinkle with the remaining grated cheese. Return the flan to the oven for 10 minutes until the cheese is golden and bubbling. Garnish with paprika and serve immediately.

CAULIFLOWER, AUBERGINE & GREEN BEAN KORMA

SERVES 4–6

INGREDIENTS

- 85 G/3 OZ CASHEW NUTS
- 1½ TBSP GARLIC AND GINGER PASTE
- 200 ML/7 FL OZ WATER
- 55 G/2 OZ GHEE OR 4 TBSP VEGETABLE OR GROUNDNUT OIL
- 1 LARGE ONION, CHOPPED
- 5 GREEN CARDAMOM PODS, LIGHTLY CRUSHED
- 1 CINNAMON STICK, BROKEN IN HALF
- ¼ TSP GROUND TURMERIC
- 250 ML/9 FL OZ DOUBLE CREAM
- 140 G/5 OZ NEW POTATOES, SCRUBBED AND CHOPPED INTO 1-CM/½-INCH PIECES
- 140 G/5 OZ CAULIFLOWER FLORETS
- ½ TSP GARAM MASALA
- 140 G/5 OZ AUBERGINE, CHOPPED INTO CHUNKS
- 140 G/5 OZ GREEN BEANS, CHOPPED INTO 1-CM/½-INCH PIECES
- SALT AND PEPPER
- CHOPPED FRESH MINT OR CORIANDER, TO GARNISH

1 Heat a large flameproof casserole or frying pan with a tight-fitting lid over a high heat. Add the cashew nuts and stir until they start to brown, then tip them out of the casserole.

2 Put the nuts in a spice blender with the garlic and ginger paste and 1 tablespoon of the water and whizz until a coarse paste forms.

3 Melt half the ghee in the casserole over a medium–high heat. Add the onion and fry for 5–8 minutes, or until golden brown. Add the nut paste and stir for 5 minutes. Stir in the cardamom pods, cinnamon stick and turmeric. Add the cream and the remaining water and bring to the boil, stirring. Reduce the heat to the lowest level, cover the casserole and simmer for 5 minutes.

4 Add the potatoes, cauliflower and garam masala to the casserole and simmer, covered, for 5 minutes. Stir in the aubergine and green beans and continue simmering for a further 5 minutes, or until all the vegetables are tender. Check the sauce occasionally to make sure it isn't sticking to the base of the casserole, and stir in extra water if needed.

5 Taste and add seasoning, if necessary. Sprinkle with the chopped mint and serve.

CHILLI BROCCOLI PASTA

SERVES 4

INGREDIENTS

- 225 G/8 OZ DRY PENNE OR MACARONI
- 225 G/8 OZ BROCCOLI
- 50 ML/2 FL OZ EXTRA VIRGIN OLIVE OIL
- 2 LARGE GARLIC CLOVES, CHOPPED
- 2 FRESH RED CHILLIES, DESEEDED AND DICED
- 8 CHERRY TOMATOES (OPTIONAL)
- SMALL HANDFUL OF FRESH BASIL OR PARSLEY, TO GARNISH

1 Bring a large saucepan of lightly salted water to the boil, add the pasta and cook for about 10 minutes, until the pasta is tender but still firm to the bite. Remove from the heat, drain, rinse with cold water and drain again. Set aside.

2 Cut the broccoli into florets. Bring a saucepan of lightly salted water to the boil, add the broccoli and cook for 5 minutes. Drain, rinse with cold water and drain again.

3 Heat the olive oil in the pan that the pasta was cooked in. Add the garlic, chillies and tomatoes, if using. Cook over a high heat for 1 minute.

4 Return the broccoli to the pan with the oil and mix well. Cook for 2 minutes to heat through. Add the pasta and mix well again. Cook for a further minute.

5 Remove the pasta from the heat, tip into a large serving bowl and serve, garnished with the basil.

SPINACH & RICOTTA GNOCCHI

SERVES 4–6

INGREDIENTS

- 1 TBSP OLIVE OIL
- 500 G/1 LB 2 OZ SPINACH LEAVES
- 225 G/8 OZ RICOTTA CHEESE
- 115 G/4 OZ PARMESAN OR PECORINO CHEESE, FRESHLY GRATED
- 2 EGGS, LIGHTLY BEATEN
- 55 G/2 OZ PLAIN FLOUR, PLUS EXTRA FOR DUSTING
- FRESHLY GRATED NUTMEG
- SALT AND PEPPER
- FRESH BASIL LEAVES, TO GARNISH
- FRESHLY GRATED PARMESAN CHEESE, TO SERVE

SAUCE

- 2 TBSP OLIVE OIL
- 2 SHALLOTS, FINELY CHOPPED
- 1 CARROT, PEELED AND FINELY DICED
- 2 GARLIC CLOVES, CRUSHED
- 800 G/1 LB 12 OZ CANNED CHOPPED TOMATOES
- 1 TBSP TOMATO PURÉE
- 6 FRESH BASIL LEAVES, ROUGHLY TORN INTO PIECES

1 Heat the oil in a large saucepan. Add the spinach and cook, covered, for 1–2 minutes until just wilted. Drain through a sieve and leave to cool, then squeeze out as much water as possible with your hands (you can squeeze it in a clean tea towel to ensure that it is very dry).

2 Finely chop the spinach and put in a bowl. Add the ricotta cheese, half the Parmesan cheese, the eggs and flour and mix well. Season to taste with salt and pepper and add a good grating of nutmeg. Cover and chill in the refrigerator for at least 1 hour.

3 Meanwhile, make the sauce. Heat the oil in a saucepan, add the shallots, carrot and garlic and cook over a medium heat, stirring frequently, for 3–4 minutes until soft. Add the tomatoes and tomato purée and bring to the boil, then reduce the heat and simmer, uncovered, for 10–15 minutes until the sauce is reduced and thickened. Season to taste with salt and pepper and add the basil leaves. If you like a smooth sauce, pass it through a sieve or process in a food processor or blender.

4 To shape the gnocchi, flour a plate and your hands thoroughly. Put a dessertspoonful of the spinach mixture into the palm of one hand, roll gently into an egg shape and transfer to a floured baking sheet. Repeat with the remaining spinach mixture.

5 Bring a large saucepan of water to a simmer, carefully add the gnocchi, in small batches, and cook gently for 2–3 minutes until they rise to the surface. Remove with a slotted spoon and transfer to a warmed serving dish to keep warm while you cook the remaining gnocchi.

6 Serve the gnocchi in warmed dishes with the sauce poured over the top, garnished with the basil leaves and with some Parmesan cheese for sprinkling.

CABBAGE & WALNUT STIR-FRY

SERVES 4

INGREDIENTS

- 350 G/12 OZ WHITE CABBAGE
- 350 G/12 OZ RED CABBAGE
- 4 TBSP GROUNDNUT OIL
- 1 TBSP WALNUT OIL
- 2 GARLIC CLOVES, CRUSHED
- 8 SPRING ONIONS, TRIMMED
- 225 G/8 OZ FIRM TOFU, CUBED
- 2 TBSP LEMON JUICE
- 100 G/3½ OZ WALNUT HALVES
- 2 TSP DIJON MUSTARD
- SALT AND PEPPER
- 2 TSP POPPY SEEDS,
  TO GARNISH

1 Using a sharp knife, thinly shred the white and red cabbages and set aside until required.

2 Heat the groundnut and walnut oils in a preheated wok. Add the garlic, cabbage, spring onions and tofu and cook for 5 minutes, stirring.

3 Add the lemon juice, walnuts and mustard to the wok and stir to combine thoroughly.

4 Season the mixture to taste with salt and pepper and cook for a further 5 minutes, or until the cabbage is tender.

5 Transfer the stir-fry to a warmed serving bowl, sprinkle with poppy seeds and serve immediately.

BRUSSELS SPROUTS WITH CHESTNUTS

SERVES 4

INGREDIENTS
- 450 G/1 LB BRUSSELS SPROUTS
- 115 G/4 OZ UNSALTED BUTTER
- 55 G/2 OZ BROWN SUGAR
- 115 G/4 OZ COOKED AND
  SHELLED CHESTNUTS

1 Trim the sprouts, removing the coarse stems and any loose outer leaves. Bring a large saucepan of lightly salted water to the boil over a high heat. Add the sprouts and boil for 5–10 minutes until just cooked but not too soft. Drain well, rinse in cold water and drain again. Set aside.

2 Melt the butter in a heavy-based frying pan. Add the sugar and stir over a medium heat until dissolved.

3 Add the chestnuts to the pan and cook, stirring occasionally, until they are well coated and starting to brown.

4 Add the sprouts to the pan with the chestnuts and mix well. Reduce the heat and cook gently, stirring occasionally, for 3–4 minutes to heat through.

5 Remove from the heat, transfer to a serving dish and serve.

WATERCRESS, COURGETTE & MINT SALAD

SERVES 4

INGREDIENTS

- 2 COURGETTES, CUT INTO BATONS
- 100 G/3½ OZ GREEN BEANS, CUT INTO THIRDS
- 1 GREEN PEPPER, DESEEDED AND CUT INTO STRIPS
- 2 CELERY STICKS, SLICED
- 1 BUNCH WATERCRESS

DRESSING
- 200 ML/7 FL OZ NATURAL YOGURT
- 1 GARLIC CLOVE, CRUSHED
- 2 TBSP CHOPPED FRESH MINT
- PEPPER

1 Bring a saucepan of lightly salted water to the boil, add the courgette batons and beans and cook for 7–8 minutes. Drain, rinse under cold running water and drain again. Set aside to cool completely.

2 Mix the courgettes and beans with the pepper strips, celery and watercress in a large serving bowl.

3 To make the dressing, combine the yogurt, garlic and mint in a small bowl. Season with pepper to taste.

4 Spoon the dressing on to the salad and serve immediately.

PAK CHOI WITH
CASHEW NUTS

SERVES 4

INGREDIENTS

- 2 RED ONIONS
- 175 G/6 OZ RED CABBAGE
- 2 TBSP GROUNDNUT OIL
- 225 G/8 OZ PAK CHOI
- 2 TBSP PLUM SAUCE
- 100 G/3½ OZ ROASTED CASHEW
  NUTS

1 Using a sharp knife, cut the red onions into thin wedges and thinly shred the red cabbage.

2 Heat the groundnut oil in a large preheated wok or heavy-based frying pan until it is really hot.

3 Add the onion wedges to the wok or frying pan and stir-fry for about 5 minutes, or until the onions are just beginning to brown.

4 Add the red cabbage to the wok and stir-fry for a further 2–3 minutes.

5 Add the pak choi leaves to the wok or frying pan and stir-fry for about 5 minutes, or until the leaves have just wilted.

6 Drizzle the plum sauce over the vegetables, toss together until well combined and heat until the liquid is beginning to bubble.

7 Scatter the roasted cashew nuts over the stir-fry and transfer to warmed serving bowls. Serve immediately.

RED CURRY WITH MIXED LEAVES

SERVES 4

INGREDIENTS

- 2 TBSP GROUNDNUT OR VEGETABLE OIL
- 2 ONIONS, THINLY SLICED
- 1 BUNCH FINE ASPARAGUS SPEARS
- 400 ML/14 FL OZ CANNED COCONUT MILK
- 2 TBSP RED CURRY PASTE
- 3 FRESH KAFFIR LIME LEAVES
- 225 G/8 OZ BABY SPINACH LEAVES
- 2 HEADS PAK CHOI, CHOPPED
- 1 SMALL HEAD CHINESE LEAVES, SHREDDED
- HANDFUL OF FRESH CORIANDER, CHOPPED
- COOKED RICE, TO SERVE

1 Heat the oil in a preheated wok, add the onions and asparagus and stir-fry over a medium–high heat for 1–2 minutes.

2 Add the coconut milk, curry paste and lime leaves and bring gently to the boil, stirring occasionally. Add the spinach, pak choi and Chinese leaves and cook, stirring, for 2–3 minutes until wilted. Add the coriander and stir well. Serve immediately with rice.

ROCKET & TOMATO RISOTTO

SERVES 4–6

INGREDIENTS

- 2 TBSP OLIVE OIL
- 2 TBSP UNSALTED BUTTER
- 1 LARGE ONION, FINELY CHOPPED
- 2 GARLIC CLOVES, FINELY CHOPPED
- 350 G/12 OZ ARBORIO RICE
- 125 ML/4 FL OZ DRY WHITE VERMOUTH
- 1.5 LITRES/2¾ PINTS VEGETABLE STOCK, SIMMERING (SEE PAGE 36)
- 6 VINE-RIPENED OR ITALIAN PLUM TOMATOES, DESEEDED AND CHOPPED
- 125 G/4½ OZ WILD ROCKET
- HANDFUL OF FRESH BASIL LEAVES
- 115 G/4 OZ FRESHLY GRATED PARMESAN CHEESE
- 225 G/8 OZ FRESH ITALIAN BUFFALO MOZZARELLA, COARSELY GRATED OR DICED
- SALT AND PEPPER

1 Heat the oil and half the butter in a large frying pan. Add the onion and cook for about 2 minutes until just beginning to soften. Stir in the garlic and rice and cook, stirring frequently, until the rice is translucent and well coated.

2 Pour in the vermouth; it will evaporate almost immediately. Add a ladleful of the stock and cook, stirring, until it is absorbed.

3 Continue adding the stock, about half a ladleful at a time, allowing each addition to be absorbed before adding the next. Just before the rice is tender, stir in the chopped tomatoes and rocket. Shred the basil leaves and immediately stir into the risotto. Continue to cook, adding more stock, until the risotto is creamy and the rice is tender, but firm to the bite.

4 Remove from the heat and stir in the remaining butter, and the grated Parmesan and mozzarella cheeses. Season to taste with salt and pepper. Remove the pan from the heat, cover and leave to stand for about 1 minute. Serve immediately, before the mozzarella melts completely.